IAPP CIPP/US Certification

A Practical Study Guide to Master the Certified Information Privacy Professional Exam

Copyright 2024 Jamie Murphy- All rights reserved.

In no way is it legal to reproduce, duplicate, or transmit any part of this document in either electronic means or in printed format. Recording of this publication is strictly prohibited and any storage of this document is not allowed unless with written permission from the publisher. All rights reserved.

The information provided herein is stated to be truthful and consistent, in that any liability, in terms of inattention or otherwise, by any usage or abuse of any policies, processes, or directions contained within is the solitary and utter responsibility of the recipient reader. Under no circumstances will any legal re- sponsibility or blame be held against the publisher for any reparation, damages, or monetary loss due to the information herein, either directly or indirectly.
Respective authors own all copyrights not held by the publisher.

Legal Notice:

This book is copyright protected. This is only for personal use. You cannot amend, distribute, sell, use, quote or paraphrase any part or the content within this book without the consent of the author or copyright owner. Legal action will be pursued if this is breached.

Disclaimer Notice:

Please note the information contained within this document is for educational and entertainment purposes only. Every attempt has been made to provide accurate, up to date and reliable complete information. No warranties of any kind are expressed or implied. Readers acknowledge that the author is not engaging in the rendering of legal, financial, medical or professional advice.

By reading this document, the reader agrees that under no circumstances are we responsible for any loss- es, direct or indirect, which are incurred as a result of the use of information contained within this document, including, but not limited to, —errors, omissions, or inaccuracies

Table of Contents

Introduction

At the forefront of this critical field stands the Certified Information Privacy Professional/United States (CIPP/US) credential, a globally recognized benchmark demonstrating a deep understanding of U.S. privacy laws and regulations. This book serves as your roadmap to CIPP/US certification success, equipping you with the knowledge, strategies, and practice tools necessary to conquer the exam and embark on a rewarding career as a privacy professional.

The CIPP/US Exam: Demystifying the Gateway to Privacy Expertise

Offered by the International Association of Privacy Professionals (IAPP), the CIPP/US exam is a computer-based test consisting of 100 multiple-choice questions delivered within a 120-minute timeframe. A score of 70% or higher is required to achieve the coveted CIPP/US designation.

CIPP/US Exam Certification: More Than Just a Piece of Paper

Earning the CIPP/US certification signifies far more than simply passing an exam. It represents:

Expertise: Demonstrating a comprehensive understanding of U.S. federal and state privacy laws, regulations, and best practices.

Credibility: Bolstering your reputation as a trusted advisor and enhancing your professional standing in the eyes of colleagues, clients, and stakeholders.

Career Advancement: Opening doors to exciting opportunities in the dynamic field of privacy, with potential for increased earning potential and career growth.

Exam Objective Map: Charting Your Course to Success

The CIPP/US exam delves into seven core domains, each encompassing various objectives that are meticulously evaluated through the test questions. This Exam Objective Map provides a high-level overview of these crucial areas:

Domain 1: Introduction to U.S. Privacy Environment

Comprehending key privacy principles and stakeholders involved in the U.S. privacy landscape.

Understanding the historical development of U.S. privacy laws and regulations.

Domain 2: Limits on Private-Sector Collection and Use of Data

Grasping the legal and ethical limitations on data collection, use, and disclosure by private organizations.

Understanding the Fair Information Practices Principles (FIPPs) and their application in various contexts.

Domain 3: Government and Court Access to Private-Sector Information

Acquiring knowledge of legal mechanisms like warrants, subpoenas, and national security letters employed by the government to access private information.

Understanding the Fourth Amendment and its implications for privacy rights in the digital age.

Domain 4: Workplace Privacy

Grasping the legal framework governing employee monitoring, data breaches, and other privacy concerns in the workplace.

Understanding the interplay between federal and state laws in the context of workplace privacy.

Domain 5: State Privacy Laws

Gaining knowledge of key state privacy laws, such as the CCPA and VCDPA, and their respective requirements for data protection.

Understanding the evolving landscape of state privacy legislation and its impact on organizations operating across various jurisdictions.

Domain 6: International Considerations for U.S. Businesses

Examining the impact of international privacy laws, like the GDPR, on U.S. businesses with global operations.

Understanding the challenges and opportunities associated with compliance with international privacy frameworks.

Domain 7: Privacy Program Management and Best Practices

Acquiring the knowledge and skills necessary to develop, implement, and manage effective privacy programs within organizations.

Understanding leading practices for data governance, risk management, and incident response in the context of privacy.

The Assessment Test: Putting Your Knowledge to the Test

This book incorporates an Assessment Test specifically designed to assess your foundational understanding of key privacy concepts and legal frameworks. The test, presented later in this introduction, will provide valuable insights into your strengths and weaknesses, enabling you to tailor your study approach accordingly.

Answers to the Assessment Test: Unveiling the Mysteries

Following the Assessment Test, you will find detailed Answers accompanied by clear explanations. This section not only provides the correct solution but also offers valuable insights into the rationale behind these answers. This comprehensive approach empowers you to grasp the underlying principles and nuances of privacy law, solidifying your knowledge beyond mere memorization.

Beyond the Book: Embarking on Your CIPP/US Journey

This book serves as a springboard for your CIPP/US certification journey. The following chapters will delve deeper into each exam domain, providing in-depth explanations, relevant case studies, and practical examples. We will equip you with strategies for tackling various question formats, time management techniques for the exam, and essential test-taking tips to help you stay calm and focused under pressure.

Remember, the path to CIPP/US success requires dedication, commitment, and a thirst for knowledge. By diligently utilizing the resources provided in this book, actively engaging with the practice materials, and leveraging the assessment test and answer explanations, you can gain the confidence and expertise necessary to conquer the CIPP/ US exam and excel in the ever-evolving world of privacy.

So, embark on this journey with us, invest in your future, and unlock the exciting world of opportunities that await you as a certified privacy professional.

Chapter 1: Privacy in the Modern Era

Introduction to Privacy

Privacy, a fundamental human right, is deeply intertwined with our sense of self, autonomy, and dignity. It encompasses the right to control personal information, to determine who has access to it, and under what circumstances. However, the modern era, characterized by rapid technological advancements and an ever-growing digital footprint, poses significant challenges to safeguarding this vital right.

This chapter embarks on a journey to explore the concept of privacy in the modern context. We will delve into the historical evolution of privacy, examine the core principles that guide its protection, and analyze the intricate relationship between privacy and technology.

A Historical Perspective on Privacy

The concept of privacy has evolved significantly throughout history. While its origins can be traced back to ancient civilizations, the modern understanding of privacy arose during the Enlightenment period, emphasizing individual liberty and control over personal information.

The right to privacy gained further prominence in the 20th century with landmark legal cases and the formulation of key declarations. For instance, the United Nations Universal Declaration of Human Rights (UDHR) in 1948 enshrined the "right to privacy" in Article 12. Similarly, the Fourth Amendment of the U.S. Constitution protects individuals from unreasonable searches and seizures, safeguarding their privacy from government intrusion.

Generally Accepted Privacy Principles (GAPPs): A Framework for Protection

To navigate the complex landscape of privacy, several Generally Accepted Privacy Principles (GAPPs) have been established. These principles act as a guiding framework for organizations and individuals alike, fostering responsible data collection, use, and disclosure practices. Here's an overview of some key GAPPs:

Notice: Individuals have the right to be informed about the collection, use, and disclosure of their personal information.

Choice: Individuals have the right to choose whether or not to consent to the collection, use, and disclosure of their personal information.

Access: Individuals have the right to access their personal information and to correct any inaccuracies.

Security: Organizations must take appropriate measures to protect personal information from unauthorized access, alteration, disclosure, or destruction.

Accountability: Organizations are accountable for complying with privacy principles and implementing appropriate safeguards.

These GAPPs serve as a foundation for building trust and ensuring responsible data stewardship in the modern world.

The Technological Challenge: Balancing Innovation with Privacy

Technological advancements have undoubtedly revolutionized our lives, offering unprecedented convenience and connectivity. However, these innovations have also ushered in an era of unprecedented data collection and analysis.

From social media platforms to online transactions, individuals constantly generate and share personal information. This vast amount of data is collected, stored, and processed by organizations, raising concerns about potential misuse, unauthorized access, and targeted manipulation.

Challenges and Opportunities in the Digital Age

The digital age presents unique challenges to safeguarding privacy:

Transparency and control: With complex data collection practices and intricate privacy policies, individuals often lack transparency and control over how their information is used.

Data breaches and security risks: The increasing reliance on digital systems exposes personal information to the constant threat of cyberattacks and data breaches, jeopardizing individual privacy and security.

Targeted advertising and profiling: Organizations leverage personal data to create detailed profiles of individuals, enabling them to deliver targeted advertising and potentially manipulate online behavior.

Despite these challenges, the digital age also presents opportunities to enhance privacy:

Technological solutions: Advancements in encryption, anonymization, and blockchain technologies can offer innovative solutions for securing personal information and enabling individuals to regain control over their data.

Increased awareness and advocacy: Growing public awareness and advocacy efforts are driving policymakers and organizations to prioritize privacy protection and develop more robust legal frameworks.

Privacy in the modern era is a complex and evolving concept. Understanding its historical context, embracing its core principles, and acknowledging the challenges and opportunities presented by technology are crucial steps towards navigating this complex landscape. By actively advocating for privacy and engaging with technological solutions that empower individuals, we can strive towards a future where privacy and innovation coexist in harmony.

Developing a Privacy Program

Building a robust privacy program is crucial for organizations in the modern era. This program outlines a set of policies, procedures, and controls to ensure compliance with privacy laws and regulations, while also fostering a culture of privacy awareness within the organization. Here are some key aspects of developing a successful privacy program:

Conduct a Privacy Impact Assessment (PIA): This assessment identifies the types of personal information collected, the purposes of collection, and potential risks associated with its use and disclosure.

Develop and implement a Privacy Policy: This document clearly outlines the organization's data collection practices, information security measures, and individual rights regarding their data.

Appoint a Privacy Officer: Designating a dedicated individual or team as the "privacy champion" ensures accountability and promotes consistent implementation of privacy practices.

Train employees: Regular training programs are essential to educate employees about privacy principles, data handling procedures, and their roles in upholding the organization's privacy commitments.

Maintain data security controls: Implementing robust data security measures, including encryption, access controls, and incident response protocols, safeguards personal information from unauthorized access and security breaches.

By establishing a comprehensive privacy program, organizations can demonstrate their commitment to responsible data stewardship, build trust with stakeholders, and mitigate potential risks associated with non-compliance.

Online Privacy

The digital sphere presents unique challenges and opportunities in the context of privacy. Here are some key considerations:

Social media platforms: These platforms collect and analyze vast amounts of user data, raising concerns about targeted advertising, profiling, and potential exposure of personal information. Individuals should be mindful of the information they share, adjust privacy settings, and utilize platforms responsibly.

Cookies and tracking technologies: Websites use cookies and other tracking technologies to monitor user behavior and personalize content. Users can manage cookie settings on their browsers and utilize privacy-enhancing extensions to limit data collection.

Online privacy tools: Several tools and services are available to enhance online privacy, such as anonymization tools, password managers, and encrypted communication platforms. Utilizing these tools empowers individuals to exert greater control over their online presence.

Understanding online privacy concerns and employing relevant tools empowers individuals to navigate the digital world with greater awareness and control over their personal information.

Privacy and Cybersecurity

Cybersecurity and privacy are intricately interconnected. Data breaches and cyberattacks not only compromise the security of organizational systems but also expose personal information, jeopardizing individual privacy and potentially causing significant harm.

Organizations must adopt robust cybersecurity measures to safeguard personal information, including:

Implementing secure systems and applications.

Regularly patching vulnerabilities and updating software.

Employing robust access controls and data encryption.

Training employees on cybersecurity best practices.

By prioritizing cybersecurity, organizations can mitigate the risk of data breaches, protecting both their own interests and the privacy of individuals whose data they hold.

Privacy by Design

Privacy by Design (PbD) is a proactive approach to integrating privacy considerations into the design, development, and implementation of technology and business processes. This approach aims to:

Embed privacy throughout the entire lifecycle of a project.

Minimize data collection and only collect information necessary for specific purposes.

Provide individuals with control over their data and clear options for managing its collection and use.

Build trust and demonstrate transparency regarding data practices.

By adopting PbD, organizations can proactively address privacy concerns rather than attempting to address them retrospectively, fostering a culture of privacy awareness and responsible data stewardship.

Practice Question and Answers

Which of the following is NOT a core component of the concept of privacy?

A. Control over personal information

B. Freedom from intrusion

C. Right to financial compensation

D. Sense of autonomy

Answer: C

Explanation: While privacy violations can have financial consequences, the right to financial compensation is not a core component of privacy itself.

The right to privacy is explicitly stated in which of the following documents?

A. The U.S. Declaration of Independence

B. The U.S. Bill of Rights

C. The United Nations Universal Declaration of Human Rights

D. The European Union's General Data Protection Regulation (GDPR)

Answer: C

Explanation: Article 12 of the UDHR enshrines the right to privacy. While other documents touch on privacy, it's most explicitly mentioned in the UDHR.

The Fourth Amendment to the U.S. Constitution protects individuals primarily from:

A. Unlawful discrimination

B. Cruel and unusual punishment

C. Excessive government taxation

D. Unreasonable searches and seizures

Answer: D

Explanation: The Fourth Amendment is a cornerstone of privacy rights, limiting government intrusion and requiring probable cause for searches and seizures.

Which landmark legal case in the U.S. established the concept of a "right to privacy" implied within existing Constitutional rights?

A. Roe v. Wade

B. Marbury v. Madison

C. Brown v. Board of Education

D. Griswold v. Connecticut

Answer: D

Explanation: Griswold v. Connecticut affirmed an implied right to marital privacy, setting the stage for broader privacy protections.

The principle of "notice" in the context of GAPPs refers to:

A. Organizations notifying law enforcement of privacy violations

B. Individuals notifying organizations of their privacy preferences

C. Individuals being informed of how their personal information is used

D. Organizations informing their competitors of their data practices

Answer: C

Explanation: Notice is about transparency – individuals have the right to be informed about how their data will be used.

Which of the following is the BEST example of the "choice" principle?

A. Opting out of receiving marketing emails

B. Filing a lawsuit against a company for a privacy violation

C. Reporting a data breach to the authorities

D. Deleting one's social media account

Answer: A

Explanation: Opting out embodies the idea that individuals should have control over how their data is used.

Which of the following technologies poses a significant challenge to the privacy principle of "access"?

A. Virtual reality headsets

B. Blockchain ledger systems

C. Wearable fitness trackers

D. Cloud computing services

Answer: B

Explanation: Blockchain's immutability makes correcting inaccurate data difficult, challenging the idea that individuals should be able to access and correct their data.

Targeted advertising primarily leverages which of the following to personalize ads for individuals?

A. Location tracking data

B. Facial recognition data

C. Online browsing history

D. Genetic information

Answer: C

Explanation: Targeted advertising algorithms often use online browsing history to create user profiles and serve personalized ads.

Which of the following activities most directly helps individuals exercise their privacy rights?

A. Using encrypted messaging apps

B. Shopping at local small businesses

C. Regularly reviewing social media privacy settings

D. Avoiding using the internet altogether

Answer: C

Explanation: Reviewing privacy settings gives individuals direct control over who has access to their information on social media platforms.

Which of the following is an example of how technology can enhance privacy?

A. Location tracking services pinpoint a user's exact location.

B. Biometric data is used for widespread identification.

C. Encryption tools protect data from unauthorized access.

Answer: C

Explanation: Encryption scrambles data, making it unreadable to anyone who doesn't hold the decryption key. This empowers individuals to control access to their information and protects it from unauthorized access.

What is the primary focus of "Privacy by Design" (PbD)?

A. Implementing data security measures after a product is launched.

B. Integrating privacy considerations into the entire development process.

C. Prioritizing profit maximization over user privacy concerns.

D. Encouraging users to be more cautious when sharing information online.

Answer: B

Explanation: PbD aims to proactively bake privacy considerations into the design, development, and implementation of technology, fostering a culture of privacy awareness from the outset.

What is the term used to describe a situation where personal information is accidentally exposed due to a security breach?

A. Identity theft

B. Phishing attack

C. Data anonymization

D. Data breach

Answer: D

Explanation: A data breach refers to the unintended disclosure of sensitive information to unauthorized individuals or entities.

Which of the following statements accurately reflects the potential impact of data breaches on individuals?

A. Data breaches always result in financial losses for individuals.

B. Data breaches only affect individuals with poor online security practices.

C. Data breaches can have a range of negative consequences, including financial losses, reputational damage, and identity theft.

D. Data breaches are primarily a concern for businesses, not individuals.

Answer: C

Explanation: Data breaches can expose sensitive information like financial data or social security numbers, leading to various problems for individuals.

What is the term used to describe a legal claim arising from the unreasonable disclosure of private information without consent?

A. Copyright infringement

B. Public disclosure of private facts

C. Identity theft

D. Cybercrime

Answer: B

Explanation: Public disclosure of private facts is a tort claim that can be used to seek legal remedies when someone discloses private information about another individual without their consent.

What is the main purpose of the General Data Protection Regulation (GDPR)?

A. To regulate online advertising practices.

B. To set global standards for data protection and privacy.

C. To establish a framework for data security best practices.

D. To promote innovation in the technology sector.

Answer: B

Explanation: The GDPR, implemented by the European Union, is a comprehensive regulation designed to protect the personal data of individuals within the European Economic Area (EEA).

In the United States, which branch of government is responsible for enacting laws?

A. The Executive Branch

B. The Judicial Branch

C. The Legislative Branch

D. The Regulatory Branch

Answer: C

Explanation: The Legislative Branch, comprised of Congress (Senate and House of Representatives), has the power to enact laws.

What is the term used to describe the legal principle of judges using past court decisions to guide future rulings in similar cases?

A. Stare decisis

B. Judicial review

C. Common law

D. Habeas corpus

Answer: A

Explanation: Stare decisis promotes consistency and predictability in the legal system by relying on precedents set in prior cases.

What is the potential consequence of violating a privacy law or regulation?

A. Community service

B. Loss of voting rights

C. Legal liability, which could include civil and/or criminal penalties or regulatory sanctions.

D. Mandatory participation in privacy awareness seminars

Answer: C

Explanation: Legal liability encompasses various potential consequences, such as fines, damage awards, or compliance orders, depending on the specific violation and governing law.

Which of the following is NOT a common type of tort claim related to privacy violations?

A. Breach of contract

B. Intrusion upon seclusion

C. Public disclosure of private facts

D. Misappropriation of name or likeness

Answer: A

Explanation: While other options are related to privacy violations, breach of contract is a separate legal claim dealing with non-fulfillment of contractual obligations.

What is the term used to describe the unintentional failure to exercise the level of care a reasonable person would in a similar situation, potentially causing harm to others?

A. Malicious intent

B. Gross negligence

C. Negligence

D. Strict liability

Answer: C

Explanation: Negligence is a key concept in tort law, and it refers to the failure to exercise reasonable care, potentially leading to legal liability.

The increasing use of facial recognition technology raises concerns about:

A. The efficiency of online shopping experiences.

B. Potential biases embedded in the algorithms and the risk of discrimination.

C. The ease of accessing entertainment content.

D. The enjoyment of video games.

Answer: B

Explanation: Facial recognition technology raises ethical concerns regarding potential biases and discriminatory outcomes, necessitating careful consideration and potential regulation.

What is the purpose of anonymizing or pseudonymizing data?

A. To completely erase all personal information from a dataset.

B. To reduce the risk of re-identification of individuals while still enabling data analysis.

C. To simplify data storage and management processes.

D. To increase the market value of a dataset.

Answer: B

Explanation: Anonymization and pseudonymization aim to protect individual privacy by reducing the risk of re-identification while still allowing some level of data utility for research or other purposes.

What is the potential challenge associated with relying solely on anonymized data for research purposes?

A. Anonymized data is always completely secure and cannot be re-identified.

B. Anonymization techniques can be expensive and time-consuming to implement.

C. Anonymized data may still contain sensitive information that can be inferred through analysis.

D. Anonymized data is not useful for any research purposes.

Answer: C

Explanation: Even with anonymization, careful analysis or combining data sets can potentially reveal information about individuals, highlighting the need for additional safeguards.

What is the primary concern regarding the potential bias of AI algorithms in the context of privacy?

A. AI algorithms are inherently biased against certain groups of people.

B. AI algorithms are not transparent in their decision-making processes.

C. AI algorithms can perpetuate existing societal biases if not carefully designed and monitored.

D. AI algorithms are intentionally programmed to discriminate against specific groups.

Answer: C

Explanation: The issue lies in the potential for biased data or algorithms to perpetuate existing societal biases,

What is the term used to describe the collection, use, and sharing of personal information in a way that does not identify individuals directly, but could be used to infer their identity when combined with other information?

A. Aggregation

B. Pseudonymization

C. De-identification

D. Differential privacy

Answer: A

Explanation: Aggregation refers to combining data from multiple sources, potentially allowing individuals to be re-identified if not anonymized or pseudonymized effectively.

The right to be forgotten, which allows individuals to request the erasure of their personal data under certain circumstances, is enshrined in which legal framework?

A. The U.S. Federal Trade Commission Act

B. The California Consumer Privacy Act (CCPA)

C. The General Data Protection Regulation (GDPR)

D. The Health Insurance Portability and Accountability Act (HIPAA)

Answer: C

Explanation: The GDPR grants individuals the "right to be forgotten" under certain conditions, allowing them to request the erasure of their personal data.

What is the primary challenge associated with cross-border data transfers in the context of privacy?

A. The lack of internet connectivity in developing countries.

B. The varying privacy laws and regulations across different countries.

C. The difficulty of translating data into different languages.

D. The cost of data storage and security measures.

Answer: B

Explanation: The diverse legal landscape surrounding privacy across different countries creates challenges for organizations transferring data internationally, requiring adherence to potentially conflicting regulations.

What is the role of data protection authorities (DPAs) in the context of privacy enforcement?

A. To develop and maintain social media platforms.

B. To investigate and enforce compliance with privacy laws and regulations.

C. To provide legal advice to individuals on privacy matters.

D. To conduct research on emerging technologies and their impact on privacy.

Answer: B

Explanation: DPAs are independent bodies responsible for overseeing and enforcing compliance with data protection laws within their jurisdiction.

What is the main objective of privacy impact assessments (PIAs)?

A. To assess the potential financial impact of a data breach.

B. To identify and evaluate the potential risks to privacy associated with a project or technology.

C. To develop marketing strategies for new data-driven products.

D. To train employees on data security best practices.

Answer: B

Explanation: PIAs are proactive tools used to identify, assess, and mitigate potential privacy risks associated with a project, technology, or business process.

Which of the following statements accurately reflects the current state of privacy law?

A. There are currently no comprehensive privacy laws or regulations in place anywhere in the world.

B. Privacy laws are standardized and consistent across all countries.

C. The legal landscape surrounding privacy is constantly evolving, with new regulations and challenges emerging.

D. Only a limited number of countries have enacted any form of privacy legislation.

Answer: C

Explanation: Privacy law is a dynamic and evolving field, with different countries at various stages of development and enforcement of their legal frameworks.

What is the BEST practice for individuals concerned about their online privacy?

A. Avoiding the internet altogether.

B. Sharing all personal information freely on social media.

C. Regularly reviewing and adjusting privacy settings on online accounts.

D. Trusting all websites and applications with their personal information.

Answer: C

Explanation: Taking proactive steps to manage privacy settings on various platforms empowers individuals to control the information they share online.

What is the term used to describe the practice of using strong and unique passwords for different online accounts?

A. Multi-factor authentication (MFA)

B. Password rotation

C. Password encryption

D. Password hygiene

Answer: D

Explanation: Password hygiene encompasses various practices like using strong passwords, avoiding reuse, and changing them periodically.

Which of the following is NOT a recommended approach for individuals seeking to enhance their online privacy?

A. Using privacy-focused search engines.

B. Disabling location tracking on mobile devices when not in use.

C. Clicking on every link or advertisement encountered online.

D. Employing encryption tools to protect sensitive information.

Answer: C

Explanation: Clicking on suspicious links or advertisements can expose individuals to security risks and potential privacy violations.

What is the primary benefit of using privacy-enhancing extensions for web browsers?

A. They automatically generate strong and unique passwords.

B. They block tracking cookies and scripts that collect user data.

C. They guarantee complete anonymity online.

D. They improve the loading speed of websites.

Answer: B

Explanation: Privacy-enhancing extensions help individuals limit the data websites and third parties can collect through tracking mechanisms.

What is the role of staying informed about privacy issues in empowering individuals?

A. It allows individuals to avoid using technology altogether.

B. It equips individuals to make informed decisions about their online activities and data sharing.

C. It guarantees complete protection against all privacy threats.

D. It simplifies the process of managing online privacy settings.

Answer: B

Explanation: Knowledge empowers individuals to understand privacy risks and take steps to mitigate them by adjusting their online behavior and utilizing appropriate tools.

What is the core principle underlying the concept of "Privacy by Design" (PbD)?

A. Retrofitting existing technologies with privacy safeguards after they are launched.

B. Integrating privacy considerations into the design, development, and implementation of technology from the outset.

C. Prioritizing profit maximization over user privacy concerns whenever possible.

D. Encouraging users to be solely responsible for protecting their privacy online.

Answer: B

Explanation: PbD emphasizes proactive integration of privacy considerations throughout the entire development lifecycle, fostering a culture of privacy awareness.

What are some potential benefits of balancing privacy protection with technological innovation?

A. Increased opportunities for government surveillance and control.

B. Fostering trust and transparency between individuals and technology companies.

C. Limiting the development and adoption of new technologies.

D. Reducing the overall cost of data security measures.

Answer: B

Explanation: Striking a balance between privacy and innovation can foster trust, transparency, and responsible development of technologies that benefit individuals and society as a whole.

What is the term used to describe a hypothetical future scenario where individuals have little to no control over their personal data due to advancements in technology and the pervasiveness of surveillance?

A. Digital utopia

B. Privacy paradox

C. Algorithmic society

D. Data dystopia

Answer: D

Explanation: Data dystopia refers to a potential future where excessive data collection and surveillance erode individual privacy and control.

What is the role of individuals in shaping the future of privacy?

A. Completely relying on governments and corporations to address privacy concerns.

B. Engaging in informed discussions, advocating for strong privacy protections, and holding organizations accountable.

C. Avoiding the use of technology altogether to preserve privacy.

D. Trusting that technological advancements will ultimately solve all privacy challenges.

Answer: B Engaging in informed discussions, advocating for strong privacy protections, and holding organizations accountable empowers individuals to play a crucial role in shaping the future of privacy.

What is the term used to describe the gap between individuals' stated privacy concerns and their actual online behavior, where they may share more information than they express discomfort with?

A. Digital divide

B. Privacy paradox

C. Algorithmic bias

D. Filter bubble

Answer: B

Explanation: The privacy paradox highlights the discrepancy between individuals' stated concerns about privacy and their actual online behavior, where they may share more information than they initially express discomfort with.

What is the primary focus of data ethics?

A. Developing the most efficient algorithms for data analysis.

B. Ensuring the responsible collection, use, and sharing of data, considering ethical implications.

C. Maximizing profits from data-driven business models.

D. Simplifying data security compliance for organizations.

Answer: B

Explanation: Data ethics focuses on the responsible and ethical collection, use, and sharing of data, taking into account potential societal and individual impacts.

What is the role of international cooperation in addressing global privacy challenges?

A. Exacerbating existing differences in privacy regulations across countries.

B. Fostering collaboration and harmonization of approaches to privacy protection.

C. Encouraging unilateral actions by individual countries without considering global implications.

D. Prioritizing national security interests over the privacy rights of individuals.

Answer: B

Explanation: International cooperation is crucial for addressing global privacy challenges, encouraging harmonization of approaches and ensuring consistent protection for individuals regardless of their location.

What is the importance of ongoing research and development in the context of privacy?

A. To develop new technologies that bypass existing privacy regulations.

B. To find new ways to collect and monetize personal data without user consent.

C. To explore innovative solutions that balance privacy and innovation in the digital age.

D. To discourage individuals from engaging with new technologies due to privacy concerns.

Answer: C

Explanation: Continuous research and development are vital for exploring innovative solutions that uphold privacy while facilitating the responsible advancement of technology.

What does the concept of "meaningful control" over personal data entail?

A. Individuals having the ability to completely opt-out of sharing their data altogether.

B. Organizations having complete control over how they collect and use personal data.

C. Individuals having the clear and transparent ability to understand, access, correct, and control the use of their personal data.

D. Governments having sole authority over the regulation and control of personal data.

Answer: C

Explanation: Meaningful control over personal data empowers individuals to understand, access, correct, and control how their data is used, fostering transparency and accountability.

What is the primary takeaway from exploring the future of privacy?

A. Privacy is no longer achievable in the digital age.

B. Technological advancements will ultimately solve all privacy challenges.

C. Shaping the future of privacy requires continuous engagement, ethical considerations, and collaborative efforts.

D. Individuals have no control over how their data is used in the digital world.

Answer: C

Explanation: Exploring the future of privacy underscores the need for ongoing engagement, ethical considerations, and collaboration among various stakeholders to navigate a complex landscape and balance individual privacy with societal progress.

Chapter 2: The Legal Environment - Navigating the Landscape of Privacy Law

In the intricate world of privacy, understanding the legal landscape is crucial. This chapter delves into the branches of government responsible for shaping privacy laws, explores the key principles of legal interpretation, analyzes the concept of legal liability, and examines torts and negligence in the context of privacy violations.

Branches of Government: Balancing Powers and Shaping Privacy Law

The United States government operates within a system of checks and balances, with three distinct branches:

Legislative: Comprised of the bicameral Congress (Senate and House of Representatives), this branch is responsible for enacting laws, including those related to privacy.

Executive: Headed by the President, the executive branch implements and enforces laws passed by the legislature. This includes establishing regulations and enforcing privacy protections through agencies like the Federal Trade Commission (FTC) and the Department of Health and Human Services (HHS).

Judicial: Comprised of the Supreme Court and lower federal courts, the judicial branch interprets and applies laws through the judicial review process. Landmark court decisions can significantly impact the legal landscape surrounding privacy.

These branches interact in a delicate balance, influencing and shaping the legal framework surrounding privacy.

Understanding Laws: Demystifying Legal Language and Interpretation

Navigating the legal environment requires an understanding of the fundamental principles of law and legal interpretation. Here are some key concepts:

Sources of Law: Laws in the United States can originate from various sources, including:

Federal Statutes: Laws enacted by Congress.

State Statutes: Laws enacted by individual state legislatures.

Regulations: Rules and guidelines established by executive agencies to implement and enforce statutes.

Common Law: Unwritten law based on judicial precedents established through court decisions.

Legal Interpretation: Judges and legal professionals interpret the meaning and application of laws. This process involves considering the statutory language, legislative history, and relevant case law.

Precedent: Court decisions in prior cases set legal precedents that guide future decisions in similar cases. This principle of "stare decisis" helps ensure consistency and predictability in the legal system.

Understanding these foundational concepts empowers individuals to better comprehend legal documents, navigate their rights and responsibilities, and participate meaningfully in conversations surrounding privacy legislation.

Legal Liability: Understanding the Consequences of Privacy Violations

In the context of privacy, legal liability refers to the state of being legally responsible for the consequences of one's actions or inactions that violate someone else's privacy rights. This legal responsibility can lead to various consequences, including:

Civil Liability: Individuals or organizations can be sued for financial damages caused by their violation of another's privacy rights.

Criminal Liability: In some instances, privacy violations may constitute criminal offenses, resulting in fines or imprisonment.

Regulatory Liability: Organizations may face regulatory sanctions, such as fines or compliance orders, for violating privacy laws and regulations.

Understanding the potential consequences of legal liability is crucial for both individuals and organizations. It incentivizes responsible data handling practices and fosters adherence to established privacy regulations.

Torts and Negligence: Exploring Legal Remedies for Privacy Violations

Torts are civil wrongs that cause harm to an individual or organization. Negligence is a specific type of tort where damages are caused by a failure to exercise the level of care that a reasonable person would in a similar situation.

In the context of privacy, several tort claims may be relevant:

Intrusion upon seclusion: This claim arises when someone intentionally intrudes upon a person's solitude or private affairs.

Public disclosure of private facts: This claim arises when someone publicly discloses private information about another individual without their consent.

Misappropriation of name or likeness: This claim arises when someone uses another person's name or likeness for their own commercial advantage without authorization.

These tort claims can offer legal remedies to individuals whose privacy rights have been violated. However, successfully claiming a tort requires meeting specific legal elements, and legal professionals should be consulted for specific situations.

Beyond the Basics: Emerging Issues and the Evolving Legal Landscape

The legal environment surrounding privacy is constantly evolving, with new technologies and emerging challenges constantly prompting legal discussions and adjustments. Here are some ongoing considerations:

Rapid technological advancements: New technologies like facial recognition and artificial intelligence raise intricate privacy concerns, prompting debates about the need for new legal frameworks and regulations.

Data breaches and security vulnerabilities: The increasing frequency of data breaches necessitates robust legal responses and encourages organizations to invest in robust cybersecurity measures.

Balancing privacy and security: Governments grapple with finding the right balance between protecting individual privacy and ensuring national security, particularly in the context of surveillance and data collection programs.

Staying informed about these evolving trends and engaging in constructive dialogue are crucial for shaping a legal environment that protects privacy while fostering innovation and progress.

Understanding the legal environment surrounding privacy empowers individuals and organizations to navigate their rights and responsibilities in the digital age. By delving into the branches of government, exploring principles of legal interpretation, and comprehending the concept of legal liability, we gain a foundational understanding of the legal framework that governs privacy. Examining torts and negligence in the context of privacy violations equips individuals with potential legal remedies, while acknowledging the evolving nature of the legal landscape underscores the need for continuous learning and engagement.

However, navigating the intricacies of privacy law requires going beyond the basic framework outlined above. This chapter further delves into key aspects of the legal landscape, including:

Federal Privacy Laws:

The Federal Trade Commission Act (FTC Act) empowers the FTC to protect consumers from unfair or deceptive practices, including those related to privacy. This broad authority allows the FTC to investigate and enforce privacy violations through various mechanisms, including issuing cease-and-desist orders and imposing civil penalties.

The Health Insurance Portability and Accountability Act (HIPAA) Privacy Rule: This regulation safeguards the privacy of protected health information (PHI) held by covered entities like healthcare providers and health plans. It establishes specific requirements for obtaining patient consent, restricting the use and disclosure of PHI, and implementing appropriate security measures.

The Gramm-Leach-Bliley Act (GLBA) Privacy Rule: This regulation protects the privacy of non-public personal information (NPI) held by financial institutions. Similar to HIPAA, it outlines requirements for obtaining customer consent, restricting the use and disclosure of NPI, and implementing appropriate security measures.

State Privacy Laws:

The landscape of state privacy laws is constantly evolving, with several states enacting comprehensive privacy regulations like the California Consumer Privacy Act (CCPA) and the Virginia Consumer Data Protection Act (VCDPA). These laws grant individuals various rights regarding their personal information, including the right to access, correct, delete, and opt-out of the sale of their data. Understanding these state-specific regulations, particularly for organizations operating across various jurisdictions, is crucial for ensuring compliance.

Cross-Border Data Transfers:

The globalized nature of the digital world presents unique challenges in regulating the transfer of personal information across borders. The European Union's General Data Protection Regulation (GDPR) imposes strict requirements on the transfer of personal data outside the European Economic Area (EEA), necessitating compliance considerations for organizations engaging in international data transfers.

Emerging Legal Issues:

Several emerging legal issues require ongoing attention and potential legislative responses, including:

Biometric data privacy: The collection and use of biometric data, such as fingerprints and facial recognition, raise critical questions about privacy, security, and potential misuse.

Data anonymization and pseudonymization: Understanding the legal implications and limitations of anonymizing and pseudonymizing data is essential to ensure the effectiveness of these practices in protecting individual privacy.

Artificial intelligence (AI) and algorithmic bias: The potential for bias in AI algorithms and the impact on individuals necessitates legal frameworks to ensure fairness, transparency, and accountability in the development and deployment of AI technologies.

The legal environment surrounding privacy is a complex and dynamic domain. By possessing a fundamental understanding of the key concepts and ongoing issues outlined in this chapter, individuals and organizations can navigate the evolving landscape with greater awareness and responsibility. This ongoing exploration, coupled with active participation in legislative discussions and advocacy efforts, is crucial for shaping a future where privacy and innovation coexist in a balanced and sustainable manner.

Adding a dedicated section on Federal Privacy Laws: Briefly explaining the FTC Act, HIPAA, and GLBA provides readers with a basic understanding of key federal regulations.

Expanding on State Privacy Laws: Highlighting California and Virginia as examples showcases the growing trend of state-level privacy legislation.

Adding a section on Cross-Border Data Transfers: Mentioning the GDPR raises awareness of international considerations in the context of privacy law.

Discussing Emerging Legal Issues: Briefly exploring biometric data, anonymization, AI, and algorithmic bias highlights evolving areas requiring ongoing legal discussion and potential regulation.

Practice Question and Answers

Which type of law is created by legislative bodies like Congress or state legislatures?

A. Common law

B. Case law

C. Statutory law

D. Administrative law

Answer: C

Explanation: Statutory law encompasses laws passed by legislative bodies, including those that specifically address privacy regulations.

What source of privacy law derives from court rulings that set legal precedents?

A. Administrative law

B. Statutory law

C. Constitutional law

D. Case law

Answer: D

Explanation: Case law precedents created by judicial rulings play a significant role in shaping privacy protections.

Which fundamental document provides the foundation for some privacy rights in the United States?

A. Declaration of Independence

B. Bill of Rights

C. U.S. Constitution

D. Articles of Confederation

Answer: C

Explanation: The U.S. Constitution, particularly amendments like the Fourth Amendment, outline some implicit privacy rights.

What type of law is established by government agencies through regulations and guidelines?

A. Administrative law

B. Contract law

C. Constitutional law

D. Civil law

Answer: A

Explanation: Administrative law includes regulations and guidelines put forth by government agencies responsible for enforcing specific areas of law, such as privacy.

Which sector-specific privacy law is designed to protect sensitive health information?

A. FCRA (Fair Credit Reporting Act)

B. HIPAA (Health Insurance Portability and Accountability Act)

C. FERPA (Family Educational Rights and Privacy Act)

D. COPPA (Children's Online Privacy Protection Act)

Answer: B

Explanation: HIPAA establishes standards for protecting and sharing sensitive health-related information.

What tort claim involves an unreasonable intrusion into an individual's seclusion or solitude?

A. Negligence

B. Intrusion upon seclusion

C. Appropriation of name or likeness

D. False light

Answer: B

Explanation: Intrusion upon seclusion focuses on protecting an individual's right to privacy in their personal affairs or spaces.

Using someone's image or name without consent for commercial gain falls under which type of tort?

A. Intrusion upon seclusion

B. Public disclosure of private facts

C. False light

D. Appropriation of name or likeness

Answer: D

Explanation: Appropriation of name or likeness protects against unauthorized use of one's identity for commercial purposes.

Which tort covers the truthful publication of private matters that would be offensive to a reasonable person?

A. Defamation

B. Negligence

C. Misappropriation

D. Public disclosure of private facts

Answer: D

Explanation: Public disclosure of private facts, even if the information is true, can form the basis of a legal claim if the disclosure is highly offensive and not of legitimate public concern.

Placing a person in a negative or misleading light in the public eye could form the basis of which privacy tort?

A. False light

B. Misappropriation

C. Intrusion upon seclusion

D. Breach of contract

Answer: A

Explanation: False light involves portraying someone in a way that is both false and highly offensive to a reasonable person.

Which type of privacy claim usually does NOT require proof of actual harm or damages?

A. False light

B. Breach of contract

C. Intrusion upon seclusion

D. Defamation

Answer: C

Explanation: Intrusion upon seclusion often focuses on the act of intrusion itself, rather than requiring proof of specific damages.

profile picture

continue

Practice Questions (continued)

The Fair Credit Reporting Act (FCRA) primarily regulates:

A. Online advertising practices.

B. The collection and use of credit information by reporting agencies.

C. The privacy of children online.

D.** Data security measures for businesses.

Answer: B

Explanation: FCRA aims to ensure accuracy, fairness, and consumer control over their credit information.

The Children's Online Privacy Protection Act (COPPA) regulates the collection and use of personal information from:

A. All internet users.

B. Individuals over the age of 18.

C.** Children under the age of 13.

D.** Users who visit specific websites.

Answer: C

Explanation: COPPA establishes specific requirements for websites and online services that collect data from children.

Which law requires employers to obtain written consent from employees before collecting and using certain health information?

A. Family Educational Rights and Privacy Act (FERPA)

B. Health Insurance Portability and Accountability Act (HIPAA)

C.** Fair Labor Standards Act (FLSA)

D.** Americans with Disabilities Act (ADA)

Answer: B

Explanation: HIPAA safeguards sensitive health information in various contexts, including the workplace.

The California Consumer Privacy Act (CCPA) grants individuals the right to:

A. Access and delete their personal information collected by businesses.

B. Opt-out of the sale of their personal information.

C.** Sue companies for data breaches without proof of harm.

D.** Be forgotten from any online search results.

Answer: B

Explanation: CCPA gives consumers the right to opt-out of the sale of their personal information to third parties.

The General Data Protection Regulation (GDPR) is a comprehensive privacy law that applies to:

A. Businesses operating in the United States.

B. Organizations processing the personal data of individuals in the European Economic Area (EEA).

C.** Social media platforms worldwide.

D.** Websites that target users in the European Union.

Answer: B

Explanation: GDPR sets a high bar for data protection and applies to organizations processing data of individuals located in the EEA, regardless of the organization's location.

What is the term used to describe a security incident involving the unauthorized access or disclosure of sensitive personal information?

A. Data breach

B.** Identity theft

C.** Phishing attack

D.** Malware infection

Answer: A

Explanation: A data breach refers to the unintended exposure of sensitive information to unauthorized individuals or entities.

What are some potential consequences of a data breach for individuals?

A. Financial losses, reputational damage, and identity theft.

B.** Increased internet censorship.

C.** Improved data security measures by companies.

D.** Easier access to online services.

Answer: A

Explanation: Data breaches can have various negative consequences for individuals, including financial losses, reputational damage, and the risk of identity theft.

What is the role of data security measures in protecting privacy?

A. Implementing safeguards to prevent unauthorized access to personal information.

B.** Encouraging individuals to share more information online.

C.** Reducing government regulation of data collection practices.

D.** Making law enforcement investigations easier.

Answer: A

Explanation: Data security measures are crucial for preventing unauthorized access, protecting information, and mitigating privacy risks.

Which of the following is NOT a common type of data security control?

A. Encryption

B.** Password complexity requirements

C.** Data minimization practices

D.** Sharing personal information with third parties for marketing purposes

Answer: D

Explanation: Data minimization focuses on collecting and storing only the data necessary for a specific purpose, unlike option D which goes against this principle.

What is the concept of "security by design" (SecBD) concerned with?

A. Integrating security considerations into the design, development, and implementation of technology from the outset.

B. Implementing security measures only after a data breach has occurred.

C. Prioritizing profit maximization over data security investments.

D. Encouraging users to be solely responsible for protecting their data online.

Answer: A

Explanation: Security by design (SecBD) emphasizes proactive integration of security safeguards throughout the entire development lifecycle of technology, fostering a culture of data protection from the beginning.

Practice Questions (continued)

What is the role of data breach notification laws?

A. To shield organizations from legal liability in the event of a data breach.

B. To inform individuals whose personal information may have been compromised in a data breach.

C. To grant companies additional time to investigate and contain data breaches.

D. To provide financial compensation to individuals affected by a data breach.

Answer: B

Explanation: Data breach notification laws mandate organizations to inform individuals whose data might be at risk following a security incident.

What are some potential challenges associated with enforcing cybersecurity regulations?

A. Lack of public awareness about online threats.

B. Difficulty keeping regulations up-to-date with evolving technology.

C. Balancing privacy protection with national security interests.

D. All of the above.

Answer: D

Explanation: Enforcing cybersecurity regulations involves navigating various challenges, including public awareness, keeping pace with technological advancements, and balancing competing interests.

What is the primary focus of international cooperation in the context of cybersecurity?

A. Promoting unilateral actions by individual countries to address cyber threats.

B. Fostering collaboration and information sharing among nations to combat cybercrime.

C. Establishing global standards for data collection practices.

D. Limiting the development and use of encryption technologies.

Answer: B

Explanation: International cooperation is crucial in addressing global cybersecurity threats, encouraging information sharing, and developing coordinated responses.

What is the purpose of the National Institute of Standards and Technology (NIST) Cybersecurity Framework?

A. To enforce mandatory cybersecurity standards for all businesses.

B. To provide voluntary guidance and recommendations for managing cybersecurity risks.

C. To investigate and prosecute cyberattacks against critical infrastructure.

D. To advocate for increased government control over the internet.

Answer: B

Explanation: The NIST Cybersecurity Framework offers a voluntary, risk-based approach to help organizations identify, protect against, detect, respond to, and recover from cybersecurity threats.

What is the role of individuals in data security?

A. Relying solely on organizations to protect their data.

B. Practicing good cybersecurity hygiene and being mindful of online risks.

C. Demanding complete anonymity from online services.

D. Sharing personal information freely to facilitate innovation.

Answer: B

Explanation: Individuals play a vital role in data security by practicing good cyber hygiene, such as using strong passwords, being cautious about clicking on links, and understanding potential online risks.

What is the term used to describe the collection and analysis of vast amounts of data by governments or corporations to gain insights into individuals or populations?

A. Algorithmic bias

B. Dataveillance

C. Data minimization

D. Privacy paradox

Answer: B

Explanation: Dataveillance refers to the systematic collection and analysis of data, often by governments or corporations, to monitor individuals or populations.

What is a potential concern associated with the use of facial recognition technology in public spaces?

A. Difficulty distinguishing between identical twins.

B. Increased accuracy in criminal investigations.

C. Potential for discriminatory profiling and privacy violations.

D. Reduced cost of security measures.

Answer: C

Explanation: Facial recognition technology raises concerns about potential misuse, discriminatory profiling, and privacy violations, particularly when deployed in public spaces.

What is the term used to describe the potential for algorithms to perpetuate or amplify biases present in the data they are trained on?

A. Algorithmic transparency

B. Algorithmic bias

C. Data security breach

D. Net neutrality

Answer: B

Explanation: Algorithmic bias refers to the potential for algorithms to reflect and amplify biases present in the data they are trained on, leading to discriminatory outcomes.

What is the role of data ethics in addressing the challenges of the digital age?

A. Developing the most efficient algorithms for data analysis, regardless of ethical implications.

B. Ensuring fairness, accountability, and transparency in the collection, use, and sharing of data.

C. Prioritizing economic benefits over ethical considerations when making data-driven decisions.

D. Limiting the development and use of artificial intelligence (AI) technologies.

Answer: B

Explanation: Data ethics emphasizes the responsible and ethical handling of data throughout its lifecycle, considering potential societal and individual impacts.

What is the primary focus of the concept of "meaningful control" over personal data?

A. Organizations having complete control over how they collect and use personal data.

B. Individuals having the clear and transparent ability to understand, access, correct, and control the use of their personal data.

C. Governments having sole authority over the regulation and control of personal data.

D. Individuals being able to opt-out of sharing their data altogether.

Answer: B

Explanation: Meaningful control empowers individuals to understand, access, correct, and control how their data is used, fostering transparency and accountability.

Chapter 3: Regulatory Enforcement

In the ever-evolving landscape of privacy law, enforcement plays a critical role in ensuring organizations comply with regulations and protecting individual privacy rights. This chapter delves into the various entities responsible for enforcing privacy regulations, exploring the different types of enforcement mechanisms employed.

Federal Regulatory Authorities

The United States has a complex system of federal agencies with varying degrees of involvement in privacy enforcement. Here are some key players:

Federal Trade Commission (FTC): With broad authority over unfair or deceptive trade practices, the FTC plays a significant role in enforcing privacy regulations, particularly those concerning data security and consumer protection. It can investigate complaints, conduct enforcement actions, and issue guidance on privacy compliance.

Securities and Exchange Commission (SEC): Focusing on protecting investors, the SEC enforces privacy regulations related to the collection and use of personal information in the financial sector, such as the Gramm-Leach-Bliley Act (GLBA).

Department of Health and Human Services (HHS): Primarily responsible for enforcing HIPAA, the HHS oversees the protection of individual health information.

Children's Online Privacy Protection Act (COPPA) Enforcement Division (FTC): This dedicated division within the FTC enforces COPPA, which safeguards the privacy of children under 13 online.

State Regulatory Authorities

Several states have enacted their own comprehensive privacy laws, creating additional layers of enforcement complexity. These state-level authorities often work in conjunction with federal agencies to ensure coordinated enforcement efforts.

California Consumer Privacy Act (CCPA) Enforcement: The California Attorney General's Office has the authority to investigate potential CCPA violations, issue warning letters, and seek civil penalties against non-compliant businesses.

Other State Laws: Other states with comprehensive privacy laws, such as Virginia and Colorado, have established their own enforcement mechanisms within their respective Attorney General's offices.

Self-Regulatory Programs

Beyond government enforcement, some industries have adopted self-regulatory programs to establish best practices and compliance standards for privacy protection. These programs often involve industry associations developing and enforcing their own codes of conduct, fostering self-policing and promoting industry-wide ethical practices.

Examples of Self-Regulatory Programs:

Digital Advertising Alliance (DAA): This self-regulatory program offers an opt-out mechanism for consumers to control interest-based advertising based on their online browsing activity.

NAFCU Privacy Pledge: The National Association of Federal Credit Unions (NAFCU) offers a privacy pledge program where member credit unions voluntarily commit to specific privacy protections for their members.

Key Enforcement Mechanisms

Regulatory bodies employ various mechanisms to enforce privacy laws, including:

Investigations: Following complaints or upon their own initiative, regulatory authorities can investigate potential violations of privacy regulations.

Informal Resolutions: Through education and guidance, informal resolutions may be pursued to encourage compliance without resorting to formal enforcement actions.

Formal Enforcement Actions: These actions may include issuing cease-and-desist orders, imposing civil penalties, or seeking injunctive relief to prevent further violations.

Challenges in Enforcement

Effective enforcement of privacy regulations faces several challenges, including:

Rapidly evolving technology: Keeping pace with technological advancements and the emergence of new privacy risks can be difficult for regulatory bodies.

Limited resources: Enforcement agencies may face resource constraints, impacting their ability to investigate all potential violations.

Complex legal landscape: The multitude of federal and state laws, along with self-regulatory programs, can create a complex and fragmented enforcement landscape.

Regulatory enforcement plays a critical role in safeguarding privacy rights in the digital age. By understanding the various actors and mechanisms involved, individuals and organizations can gain a deeper appreciation for the complexities of privacy enforcement and the ongoing efforts to ensure responsible data practices.

Practice Questions and Answers

Which federal regulatory agency has primary jurisdiction over consumer privacy and deceptive trade practices?

A. Securities and Exchange Commission (SEC)

B. Department of Health and Human Services (HHS)

C. Federal Trade Commission (FTC)

D. Consumer Financial Protection Bureau (CFPB)

Answer: C

Explanation: The FTC plays a central role in enforcing privacy laws and protecting consumers from unfair or deceptive practices, including those relating to data security and online marketing.

Which agency enforces regulations under the Children's Online Privacy Protection Act (COPPA)?

A. Department of Justice (DOJ)

B. National Institute of Standards and Technology (NIST)

C. Federal Communications Commission (FCC)

D. Federal Trade Commission (FTC)

Answer: D

Explanation: The FTC has a dedicated COPPA Enforcement Division that investigates and enforces COPPA, safeguarding the online privacy of children.

Which regulatory body is responsible for enforcing the Health Insurance Portability and Accountability Act (HIPAA)?

A. Federal Trade Commission (FTC)

B. Department of Education

C. Food and Drug Administration (FDA)

D. Department of Health and Human Services (HHS)

Answer: D

Explanation: The Office of Civil Rights (OCR) within the HHS is tasked with enforcing HIPAA, protecting the privacy of individuals' health information.

A company that manages and processes financial data would likely fall under the enforcement jurisdiction of which regulatory agency?

A. Department of Homeland Security (DHS)

B. Securities and Exchange Commission (SEC)

C. Environmental Protection Agency (EPA)

D. Department of Labor (DOL)

Answer: B

Explanation: The SEC focuses on investor protection, making it the primary regulator for companies in the financial sector, where data privacy violations could significantly impact investors.

Which state is often at the forefront of data privacy regulation, enacting the comprehensive California Consumer Privacy Act (CCPA)?

A. California

B. New York

C. Texas

D. Florida

Answer: A

Explanation: California is a leader in U.S. privacy law, with the CCPA granting significant privacy rights to Californians and impacting businesses nationwide.

What is the first step a regulatory agency typically takes when it receives a complaint regarding a potential privacy violation?

A. Issues a cease-and-desist order.

B. Initiates a lawsuit against the company.

C. Conducts an investigation.

D. Imposes immediate fines on the company.

Answer: C

Explanation: After receiving a complaint, the agency gathers information to determine if there is evidence of a violation warranting further action.

What type of enforcement action might a regulatory agency take to require a company to immediately halt a privacy-violating practice?

A. Voluntary agreement

B. Public education campaign

C. Cease-and-desist order

D. Formal compliance audit

Answer: C

Explanation: A cease-and-desist order is a legally binding directive to immediately stop the specified practice, often used in cases of urgent privacy concerns.

Which of the following is an example of a monetary penalty that might be imposed as a result of privacy enforcement actions?

A. Jail time for employees.

B. Mandatory public apology

C. Civil fines

D. Injunctive relief

Answer: C

Explanation: Civil fines are a common tool used to deter privacy violations and hold companies accountable.

Besides addressing a specific violation, what else might a regulatory body require a company to do as part of an enforcement settlement?

A. Develop and implement a comprehensive privacy program.

B. Participate in industry self-regulatory initiatives.

C. Regularly submit to privacy audits by the agency.

D. All of the above

Answer: D

Explanation: As part of an enforcement settlement, a regulatory body may require the company to take various corrective actions, including developing and implementing a comprehensive privacy program, contributing to industry self-regulatory efforts, and submitting to regular privacy audits to ensure compliance and prevent future violations.

What is the primary purpose of self-regulatory programs in the context of privacy?

A. To replace government enforcement entirely.

B. To establish industry best practices and promote self-policing regarding privacy.

C.** To impose mandatory privacy compliance standards on all companies in the industry.

D.** To advocate for weaker privacy regulations at the government level.

Answer: B

Explanation: Self-regulatory programs aim to foster industry-wide collaboration in setting and upholding privacy standards, complementing, rather than replacing, government enforcement.

Which of the following is NOT a typical characteristic of a self-regulatory program in the privacy domain?

A. Voluntary participation by companies in the sector.

B.** Development of codes of conduct outlining privacy best practices.

C.** Enforcement mechanisms through industry associations.

D.** Directly setting binding legal requirements on companies.

Answer: D

Explanation: Unlike government regulations, self-regulatory programs are typically voluntary, relying on industry cooperation and internal enforcement mechanisms rather than legal mandates.

What is an example of a self-regulatory program related to online advertising?

A. Digital Advertising Alliance (DAA)

B.** Children's Online Privacy Protection Act (COPPA)

C.** General Data Protection Regulation (GDPR)

D.** National Institute of Standards and Technology (NIST) Cybersecurity Framework

Answer: A

Explanation: The DAA offers an opt-out mechanism for consumers to control interest-based advertising, demonstrating industry cooperation in addressing online privacy concerns.

What are some potential limitations of relying solely on self-regulatory programs to ensure privacy protection?

A. Lack of mandatory compliance and potential for uneven enforcement across the industry.

B.** High cost of developing and implementing industry-wide standards.

C.** Limited applicability to companies outside the specific industry.

D.** All of the above

Answer: D

Explanation: Self-regulatory programs may face challenges due to voluntary participation, potentially leading to uneven enforcement, limited reach, and difficulty addressing broader privacy concerns beyond the specific industry.

How can self-regulatory programs work in conjunction with government enforcement to enhance privacy protection?

A. By setting industry standards that complement and inform government regulations.

B.** By providing alternative compliance pathways to reduce regulatory burden on businesses.

C.** By weakening the need for government oversight and enforcement altogether.

D.** By shielding companies from legal consequences in case of privacy violations.

Answer: A

Explanation: Self-regulatory programs can contribute by establishing industry best practices that align with and inform government regulations, fostering a comprehensive approach to privacy protection.

What is one of the primary challenges associated with effective enforcement of privacy regulations in the digital age?

A. Keeping pace with the rapid evolution of technology and emerging privacy risks.

B.** Lack of public awareness about individual privacy rights and online risks.

C.** Limited expertise and resources within regulatory agencies.

D.** Overly complex and cumbersome legal frameworks.

Answer: A

Explanation: The dynamic nature of technology poses a constant challenge for enforcement, requiring regulatory bodies to adapt and update their approaches to address new risks and online practices.

What is the role of international cooperation in addressing privacy challenges in the digital age?

A. Fostering collaboration and information sharing among nations to tackle global privacy concerns.

B.** Promoting unilateral actions by individual countries without considering international implications.

C.** Discouraging countries from setting strong privacy standards that could hinder global trade.

D.** Limiting the development and use of data-driven technologies due to privacy concerns.

Answer: A

Explanation: International cooperation is crucial for addressing global privacy issues, such as data breaches and cross-border data flows, necessitating information exchange and coordinated enforcement efforts.

What are some potential benefits of strengthening individual control over personal data?

A. Empowering individuals to understand, access, correct, and control the use of their personal data, fostering transparency and accountability.

B. Enabling organizations to collect and use more personal data without restrictions.

C. Reducing the need for government regulation and oversight of data practices.

D. Limiting the availability of data for research and innovation purposes.

Answer: A

Explanation: Giving individuals more control over their data empowers them to make informed choices, promotes transparency in data use, and holds organizations accountable for responsible data handling.

What is one potential concern associated with the concept of "data portability"?

A. Increased complexity for organizations in managing data requests from individuals.

B. Potential for data inaccuracies or inconsistencies when transferred between systems.

C. Reduced incentives for organizations to invest in data security measures.

D. All of the above

Answer: D

Explanation: Data portability, while empowering individuals, presents challenges for organizations regarding data management complexity, potential inaccuracies during transfer, and ensuring continued security practices.

What is the role of technological advancements in addressing privacy challenges?

A. Replacing the need for legal and regulatory frameworks altogether.

B. Providing tools and solutions for individuals to manage their privacy settings more effectively.

C. Making data collection and analysis easier and more efficient for organizations, potentially neglecting privacy considerations.

D. Limiting individual access to online services and platforms due to privacy concerns.

Answer: B

Explanation: Technological advancements can offer tools for individuals to manage their privacy settings, such as privacy dashboards and data access portals, while still requiring legal and ethical considerations.

What is the importance of ongoing public discourse and education about privacy issues in the digital age?

A. Raising public awareness about online threats and empowering individuals to make informed choices.

B. Encouraging individuals to share more personal information online to facilitate innovation.

C. Shifting the responsibility for privacy protection solely to governments and regulatory agencies.

D. Discouraging the development and use of new technologies due to privacy concerns.

Answer: A

Explanation: Public discourse and education play a vital role in promoting awareness about online threats and empowering individuals to understand and exercise their privacy rights effectively.

Chapter 4: Information Management

In today's digitally driven world, information is a critical asset for organizations of all sizes. Effective information management ensures the organization collects, stores, protects, and utilizes its data responsibly and efficiently. This chapter delves into five fundamental pillars of information management: Data Governance, Workforce Training, Cybersecurity Threats, Incident Response, and Vendor Management.

1. Data Governance

Data governance establishes a framework for managing an organization's information assets effectively. It defines clear roles, responsibilities, and processes for data management across the organization.

Key Components of Data Governance:

Data ownership: Clearly defining who owns and is accountable for specific data sets within the organization.

Data quality: Implementing processes to ensure data accuracy, completeness, and consistency.

Data security: Establishing measures to protect data from unauthorized access, use, disclosure, disruption, modification, or destruction.

Data privacy: Ensuring compliance with relevant privacy regulations and respecting individual data privacy rights.

Data accessibility: Defining who has access to specific data and establishing procedures for requesting and granting access.

Data retention: Determining how long to retain data based on legal, regulatory, and business requirements.

Benefits of Data Governance:

Improved data quality: Ensures data accuracy, consistency, and reliability, leading to better decision-making.

Enhanced data security: Reduces the risk of data breaches and unauthorized access.

Increased regulatory compliance: Helps organizations meet the data privacy and security requirements of various regulations.

Optimized data usage: Enables organizations to leverage data effectively for improved efficiency, innovation, and competitive advantage.

2. Workforce Training

Empowering employees with the knowledge and skills to handle information securely and responsibly is crucial for effective information management.

Training Topics:

Data security awareness: Educating employees about common cyber threats, phishing attempts, and best practices for protecting data, including password hygiene and secure browsing habits.

Data privacy principles: Training employees on relevant privacy regulations and their responsibilities regarding data collection, use, and disclosure.

Data classification and handling: Equipping employees with knowledge on identifying and classifying sensitive data according to its level of confidentiality, integrity, and availability.

Reporting procedures: Establishing clear procedures for employees to report suspected data breaches or security incidents.

Benefits of Workforce Training:

Reduced risk of human error: Educated employees are less likely to fall victim to phishing attacks or mishandle sensitive data inadvertently.

Enhanced compliance: Empowers employees to comply with data privacy regulations and organizational policies.

Improved data stewardship: Fosters a culture of data responsibility and accountability among employees.

3. Cybersecurity Threats

Organizations face a constant barrage of cybersecurity threats, making it crucial to understand the potential risks and implement safeguards to mitigate them.

Common Cybersecurity Threats:

Malware: Malicious software, including viruses, worms, and ransomware, designed to disrupt, damage, or steal data.

Phishing attacks: Deceptive emails or messages designed to trick individuals into revealing personal information or clicking on malicious links.

Social engineering: Techniques used to manipulate individuals into sharing sensitive information or granting unauthorized access to systems.

Denial-of-service (DoS) attacks: Overwhelming a system with traffic to render it unavailable to legitimate users.

Zero-day attacks: Exploiting previously unknown vulnerabilities in software or systems.

Strategies to Mitigate Cybersecurity Threats:

Implementing firewalls and intrusion detection systems: These tools monitor network traffic and identify suspicious activity.

Regularly updating software and patching vulnerabilities: Applying security updates promptly is critical to address known vulnerabilities.

Using strong passwords and enabling multi-factor authentication (MFA): Adding an extra layer of security to access control.

Back up data regularly and implement disaster recovery plans: Ensuring data recovery capabilities in case of a cyberattack or other disruptions.

4. Incident Response

Having a well-defined incident response plan is essential for effectively responding to cybersecurity incidents and minimizing their impact.

Steps of an Incident Response Plan:

Preparation: Developing policies and procedures for identifying, containing, investigating, and recovering from incidents.

Detection and Identification: Utilizing security tools and monitoring systems to detect suspicious activity and identify the nature of the incident.

Containment and Eradication: Taking immediate steps to stop the attack, isolate the affected systems, and prevent further damage.

Investigation: Determining the root cause of the incident, identifying the scope of the breach, and assessing the impact.

Recovery: Restoring affected systems and data from backups, ensuring all vulnerabilities are addressed to prevent similar incidents in the future.

4. Incident Response

Benefits of a Robust Incident Response Plan:

Minimized damage: Prompt and coordinated response helps limit the impact of an incident and speed up recovery.

Improved decision-making: A clear plan provides a framework for making informed decisions during the critical stages of an incident.

Reduced legal and regulatory risks: A documented response plan demonstrates due diligence and can help mitigate legal and regulatory repercussions.

Enhanced employee and customer confidence: A well-managed incident response fosters trust and confidence by demonstrating the organization's commitment to protecting data and responding swiftly to breaches.

5. Vendor Management

Organizations often rely on third-party vendors to provide various services, including data storage, processing, and analytics. This reliance necessitates effective vendor management to ensure the security and privacy of the organization's data.

Key Aspects of Vendor Management:

Vendor selection: Conducting thorough due diligence to assess the vendor's security posture, data privacy practices, and compliance with relevant regulations.

Contractual safeguards: Incorporating clear and comprehensive clauses in contracts that address data security, privacy, and incident response responsibilities.

Ongoing monitoring and assessment: Regularly evaluating the vendor's security controls and compliance practices to ensure continued data protection.

Benefits of Effective Vendor Management:

Reduced risk of data breaches: Thorough vetting of vendors and contractual safeguards minimize the risk of data exposure through third-party vulnerabilities.

Enhanced regulatory compliance: Demonstrates accountability for data entrusted to vendors and assists in meeting compliance obligations.

Improved information security posture: Collaborative efforts with vendors can strengthen the overall security environment of the organization.

Effective information management requires a comprehensive approach that integrates these five pillars: data governance, workforce training, cybersecurity awareness, incident response planning, and robust vendor management. By establishing clear policies, processes, and controls, organizations can ensure responsible data handling, mitigate risks, and leverage information as a valuable asset to achieve their business objectives. This chapter has provided an overview of these critical elements, but further exploration and understanding of specific aspects are recommended to tailor information management practices to the unique needs and context of each organization.

Practice Questions and Answers

1. What is the primary purpose of data governance?

A. To provide access to data for all employees regardless of their role.

B. To define clear roles, responsibilities, and processes for managing data effectively.

C. To implement the latest data analytics tools and technologies.

D. To maximize data storage capacity within the organization.

Answer: B

Explanation: Data governance establishes a framework for managing an organization's information assets effectively, ensuring clarity in data ownership, quality, security, privacy, accessibility, and retention.

2. Which of the following is NOT a benefit of data governance?

A. Increased regulatory compliance

B. Improved data security

C. Enhanced data accessibility for unauthorized users

D. Reduced risk of human error

Answer: C

Explanation: Data governance aims to restrict unauthorized access and ensure data protection, making option C incorrect.

3. What is the most critical step in an incident response plan?

A. Assigning blame for the incident.

B. Identifying the root cause of the incident.

C. Restoring affected systems and data immediately.

D. Implementing new security software on all devices.

Answer: B

Explanation: Identifying the root cause allows for targeted solutions and prevents future occurrences. Option A is unproductive, C might be premature, and D addresses prevention, not response.

4. What type of training is most relevant to information security awareness?

A. Training on the latest data analysis techniques.

B. Training on effective communication skills for presentations.

C. Training on identifying and reporting suspicious emails.

D. Training on leadership principles for managing teams.

Answer: C

Explanation: Information security awareness training educates employees to recognize and report potential cyber threats, making option C the most relevant choice.

5. When selecting a third-party vendor, what is the most crucial factor to consider regarding information management?

A. The vendor's reputation for providing excellent customer service.

B. The vendor's competitive pricing options.

C. The vendor's security controls and compliance practices.

D. The vendor's experience in the specific industry.

Answer: C

Explanation: When entrusting data to a vendor, evaluating their security and compliance practices is essential to ensure data protection, making option C the most crucial factor.

6. What is the primary goal of a strong password policy within data governance?

A. To simplify the login process for employees.

B. To encourage password sharing among colleagues.

C. To discourage frequent password changes.

D. To require complex and unique passwords for increased security.

Answer: D

Explanation: Strong password policies aim to prevent unauthorized access by requiring complex and unique combinations, making option D the primary goal.

7. Which organizational role is typically responsible for data ownership within the framework of data governance?

A. Information technology (IT) department

B. Data analysts and scientists

C. Department heads and managers

D. Chief Executive Officer (CEO)

Answer: C

Explanation: Data ownership often falls on department heads or managers who are accountable for the specific data sets used within their respective departments.

8. What is the main purpose of conducting regular vulnerability assessments as part of cybersecurity measures?

A. To demonstrate compliance with data privacy regulations.

B. To identify and address potential security weaknesses in systems.

C. To train employees on the latest hacking techniques.

D. To implement the newest security software on all devices.

Answer: B

Explanation: Vulnerability assessments proactively identify weaknesses in systems, allowing for timely patching and mitigation of potential threats, making option B the primary purpose.

9. What is the main benefit of multi-factor authentication (MFA) in information security?

A. It eliminates the need for passwords altogether.

B. It provides a single point of access for all applications.

C. It adds an extra layer of security to verify legitimate user access.

D. It automatically updates software applications with security patches.

Answer: C

Explanation: MFA requires additional verification beyond a password, such as a code sent to a mobile device, adding a significant layer of security to user access, making option C the main benefit.

10. Which of the following statements is most accurate regarding data retention policies within data governance?

A. Data should be retained indefinitely for future reference.

B. Data retention periods should be established based on legal and business requirements.

C. Data should be deleted as soon as it becomes outdated.

B. Data retention periods should be established based on legal and business requirements.**

Explanation: Data retention policies are crucial practices within data governance. These policies define how long specific data types are retained, considering both legal obligations (e.g., financial records) and business needs (e.g., customer purchase history for marketing purposes). Indefinitely holding data (A) creates unnecessary storage burden and potential security risks, while immediate deletion (C) could violate regulations or hinder valuable analyses. While organizations might have standard retention periods, specific legal cases or ongoing investigations might necessitate extended data storage (D) beyond the defined timeframe.

11. What is the primary objective of an organization's data classification scheme within data governance?

A. To categorize data based on its format (e.g., text, image).

B. To group data based on its relevance to specific projects.

C. To establish different access levels for various data types based on their sensitivity.

D. To assign ownership of specific data sets to individual employees.

Answer: C

Explanation: Data classification categorizes data based on its sensitivity (e.g., confidential, public) to determine appropriate security measures and access controls. While format (A) might be relevant for storage purposes, project relevance (B) is temporary and ownership (D) is a separate aspect of data governance.

12. What is the most effective way to encourage a culture of data security awareness within an organization?

A. Implementing strict disciplinary measures for data breaches.

B. Providing ongoing training and education programs for employees.

C. Offering financial rewards for identifying security vulnerabilities.

D. Restricting employee access to all non-essential data.

Answer: B

Explanation: While consequences exist for breaches, fostering a culture of awareness through ongoing training (B) empowers employees to identify and report threats, promoting collective responsibility and proactive security practices. Option A can create fear and hinder communication, C might incentivize false positives, and D could hinder productivity.

13. When reporting a suspected data breach, which of the following should be the top priority for an employee?

A. Identifying the specific cause of the breach.

B. Immediately notifying their manager or supervisor.

C. Gathering evidence and documenting the incident details.

D. Attempting to resolve the issue independently.

Answer: B

Explanation: Promptly notifying the appropriate authorities (B), typically the manager or designated security personnel, allows for swift investigation and response, minimizing potential damage. Identifying the cause (A) and gathering evidence (C) are crucial but come after initial reporting. Independent resolution attempts (D) could worsen the situation.

14. What is the main benefit of conducting regular penetration testing as part of an organization's cybersecurity strategy?

A. To fulfill compliance requirements for specific regulations.

B. To simulate real-world cyberattacks and identify potential vulnerabilities.

C. To showcase the organization's commitment to data security to potential customers.

D. To train employees on how to respond to actual cyberattacks.

Answer: B

Explanation: Penetration testing (pen testing) proactively simulates cyberattacks by ethical hackers, uncovering security weaknesses before they can be exploited by malicious actors. While pen testing might be required for some regulations (A), its primary benefit is vulnerability identification (B). Option C focuses on marketing, and D is a separate training objective.

15. What is the most relevant factor to consider when evaluating the effectiveness of a vendor's security controls as part of vendor management?

A. The vendor's reputation for excellent customer service.

B. The vendor's competitive pricing options for their services.

C. The existence of industry-recognized security certifications held by the vendor.

D. The length of time the vendor has been in business.

Answer: C

Explanation: Industry-recognized security certifications (C) demonstrate a vendor's commitment to robust security practices and adherence to established standards, making it the most relevant factor during evaluation. While factors like reputation (A) and pricing (B) might be relevant, they don't directly address security measures. Length of experience (D) doesn't guarantee effective security practices.

Chapter 5: Private Sector Data Collection

In today's digital age, personal data is collected by a vast array of private sector entities, from social media platforms and e-commerce websites to financial institutions and healthcare providers. While this data collection fuels innovation and facilitates various services, it also raises concerns about privacy and potential misuse. This chapter explores the legal frameworks and regulations governing private sector data collection in the United States, focusing on key areas like:

FTC Privacy Protection: The Federal Trade Commission (FTC) plays a central role in safeguarding consumer privacy. This section delves into the FTC's authority and relevant regulations, including the Children's Online Privacy Protection Act (COPPA) and the Gramm-Leach-Bliley Act (GLBA) Safeguards Rule.

Medical Privacy: The Health Insurance Portability and Accountability Act (HIPAA) establishes safeguards to protect the privacy of individuals' medical information. This section explores patients' rights under HIPAA and the responsibilities of healthcare providers regarding data handling.

Financial Privacy: The Gramm-Leach-Bliley Act (GLBA) protects consumer financial information. This section examines the requirements of GLBA, including the Fair Credit Reporting Act (FCRA) and its impact on credit reporting agencies.

Educational Privacy: The Family Educational Rights and Privacy Act (FERPA) governs the privacy of student educational records. This section explores students' and parents' rights under FERPA and the limitations on access to student records.

Telecommunication and Marketing Privacy: The Telephone Consumer Protection Act (TCPA) and the CAN-SPAM Act regulate telemarketing and email marketing practices. This section examines these regulations and their impact on how companies can contact consumers.

5.1 FTC Privacy Protection

The Federal Trade Commission (FTC) serves as the primary regulator of commercial data collection practices in the United States. The FTC enforces various laws and regulations aimed at protecting consumer privacy, including:

Children's Online Privacy Protection Act (COPPA): This law restricts the online collection and use of personal information from children under 13. It requires websites and online services to obtain verifiable parental consent before collecting, using, or disclosing children's information.

Gramm-Leach-Bliley Act (GLBA) Safeguards Rule: This rule requires financial institutions to implement and maintain a comprehensive information security program to protect the privacy and security of customer financial information.

The FTC also enforces a number of general principles regarding data collection practices, including:

Notice and Consent: Consumers have the right to be informed about what data is being collected about them, how it will be used, and with whom it will be shared. They also have the right to consent to the collection and use of their data.

Choice: Consumers should have choices regarding the collection, use, and disclosure of their data. This may include the ability to opt-out of data collection or to choose how their data is used.

Access and Correction: Consumers should have the right to access their personal information and to correct any inaccuracies.

Accountability: Companies are responsible for the security and privacy of the personal information they collect about consumers.

5.2 Medical Privacy

The Health Insurance Portability and Accountability Act (HIPAA) safeguards the privacy of individuals' medical information.

Key Features of HIPAA:

Protected Health Information (PHI): HIPPA defines specific types of information as PHI, such as a patient's medical history, diagnoses, and treatment information.

Patient Rights: HIPAA grants patients specific rights regarding their PHI, including the right to access, amend, and request an accounting of disclosures of their PHI.

Covered Entities: HIPAA applies to healthcare providers, health plans, and healthcare clearinghouses that transmit standard healthcare transactions electronically.

5.3 Financial Privacy

The Gramm-Leach-Bliley Act (GLBA) protects consumer financial information. This law includes various regulations, such as:

The Fair Credit Reporting Act (FCRA): This act regulates credit reporting agencies and ensures the accuracy, fairness, and privacy of consumer credit information. It provides consumers with the right to access their credit reports and to dispute any errors.

The Privacy Rule and the Safeguards Rule: These rules require financial institutions to implement and maintain comprehensive privacy and security programs to protect customer financial information.

5.4 Educational Privacy

The Family Educational Rights and Privacy Act (FERPA) governs the privacy of student educational records.

Key Provisions of FERPA:

Parental Rights: Parents of students under 18, and students 18 or older, have the right to access most of their educational records.

School Responsibilities: Schools must have written policies and procedures regarding the release of student educational records and must obtain consent from parents or eligible students before disclosing such information.

Exceptions to FERPA:

There are certain exceptions to FERPA where schools may disclose student educational records without consent, such as:

To other school officials who have a legitimate educational interest in the information.

To certain government officials, such as in response to a subpoena.

To parents of other students if the information is related to the safety and well-being of the student or other students.

In certain health and safety emergencies.

5.5 Telecommunication and Marketing Privacy

Regulations govern telemarketing and email marketing practices to protect consumers from unwanted and intrusive communications.

Telephone Consumer Protection Act (TCPA): This act restricts telemarketing calls and text messages to residential phone lines. It requires companies to obtain prior written consent from consumers before contacting them using automated dialing systems or prerecorded voice messages.

Controlling the Assault of Non-Solicited Pornography and Marketing Act (CAN-SPAM Act): This act establishes requirements for commercial email marketing. It requires companies to identify themselves in the email header, offer an unsubscribe option, and comply with unsubscribe requests within a reasonable timeframe.

Challenges of Private Sector Data Collection

Despite existing regulations, the constantly evolving digital landscape presents ongoing challenges in private sector data collection:

Rapid Technological Advancements: New technologies and data collection methods constantly emerge, requiring continual updates to regulations and enforcement strategies.

Data Aggregation and Secondary Use: Combining data from various sources can create detailed profiles of individuals, raising concerns about potential misuse and the difficulty of obtaining informed consent for all potential uses.

Cross-Border Data Flows: Data collected in one country may be transferred and stored in another, creating jurisdictional complexities and potential privacy risks in countries with less stringent regulations.

Private sector data collection offers numerous benefits, but it also raises complex privacy concerns. Understanding the legal frameworks and regulations governing data collection practices in the United States is crucial for both companies and individuals. Continued dialogue and adaptation are necessary to balance the benefits of data-driven innovation with the fundamental right to privacy in the digital age.

Practice Question and Answers

Which of the following laws provides specific protections for children's online information?

A. CAN-SPAM Act

B. Gramm-Leach-Bliley Act (GLBA)

C. Children's Online Privacy Protection Act (COPPA)

D. Fair Credit Reporting Act (FCRA)

Answer: C

Explanation: COPPA specifically regulates the collection of data from children under 13 by websites and online services, mandating parental consent.

What is a fundamental principle enforced by the Federal Trade Commission (FTC) regarding consumer privacy?

A. Notice and consent

B. Minimization of data analysis

C. Mandatory data encryption

D. Total restriction on data collection

Answer: A

Explanation: The principle of notice and consent means consumers should be informed about what information is collected, how it's used, and have the opportunity to consent or opt-out.

Which FTC regulation within the Gramm-Leach-Bliley Act (GLBA) emphasizes the protection of consumer financial data?

A. Safeguards Rule

B. Privacy Rule

C. Fair Credit Reporting Act (FCRA)

D. Children's Online Privacy Protection Act (COPPA)

Answer: A

Explanation: The GLBA Safeguards Rule mandates financial institutions to implement security measures to protect sensitive customer information.

HIPAA applies to which of the following entities?

A. Healthcare providers

B. Social media companies

C. Retail stores

D. All of the above

Answer: A

Explanation: HIPAA directly regulates healthcare providers, health plans, and healthcare clearinghouses that transmit electronic health transactions.

Under HIPAA, what is considered Protected Health Information (PHI)?

A. A patient's diagnosis and treatment details

B. A person's favorite ice cream flavor

C. A celebrity's shopping habits

D. A company's financial records

Answer: A

Explanation: PHI refers to individually identifiable health information, including medical history, test results, and other health-related data.

Which of the following is a patient right granted by HIPAA?

A. To access and amend their medical records

B. To sell their own medical information for profit

C. To disclose a friend's health information without consent

D. To have their healthcare provider delete their medical records

Answer: A

Explanation: HIPAA gives patients the right to access their medical records, request corrections, and receive an accounting of certain disclosures of their PHI.

What does the Gramm-Leach-Bliley Act (GLBA) aim to protect?

A. Customer financial information

B. Children's online activities

C. Unsolicited email marketing

D. Educational records

Answer: A

Explanation: GLBA focuses on the confidentiality and security of non-public personal financial information held by financial institutions.

The Fair Credit Reporting Act (FCRA) is a key component of which broader regulation?

A. CAN-SPAM Act

B. Gramm-Leach-Bliley Act

C. HIPAA

D. FERPA

Answer: B

Explanation: The FRCA is part of the GLBA and ensures fairness and accuracy for individuals whose information is used by consumer reporting agencies.

Under the FCRA, what right does a consumer have if they find an error in their credit report?

A. To file a lawsuit against the creditor

B. To erase the negative information

C. To dispute the information and have it corrected

D. To change their credit score instantly

Answer: C

Explanation: The FCRA allows consumers to challenge inaccurate information on their credit reports and have it investigated and corrected, if necessary.

Which law governs the privacy of student educational records?

A. TCPA

B. HIPAA

C. FERPA

D. COPPA

Answer: C

Explanation: FERPA specifically addresses the disclosure and protection of student education records.

11. Who has the right to access a student's educational records under FERPA?

* A. The student's teacher without permission

* B. Anyone who requests the information online

* C. The student's parents or eligible students (over 18)

* D. The student's friends with parental consent

Answer: C**

Explanation: FERPA grants access rights to students over 18 and their parents of students under 18, with exceptions for specific situations outlined in the law.

12. What is an example of an exception to FERPA where a school may disclose student records without consent?

* A. To share the student's grades with a potential employer

* B. To promote the school's academic achievements

* C. To report suspected child abuse to authorities

* D. To sell the student's contact information to marketing companies

Answer: C**

Explanation: FERPA allows exceptions for reporting suspected child abuse or neglect to mandated reporters, ensuring the safety and well-being of children.

Telecommunication and Marketing Privacy

13. What act restricts telemarketing calls and text messages to residential phone lines?

* A. GLBA Safeguards Rule

* B. FCRA

* C. Telephone Consumer Protection Act (TCPA)

* D. CAN-SPAM Act

Answer: C**

Explanation: The TCPA aims to protect consumers from unwanted telemarketing calls and text messages by requiring prior written consent for automated dialing systems or prerecorded messages.

14. Which act regulates the sending of commercial emails?

* A. TCPA

* B. FERPA

* C. HIPAA

* D. Controlling the Assault of Non-Solicited Pornography and Marketing Act (CAN-SPAM Act)

Answer: D**

Explanation: The CAN-SPAM Act establishes guidelines for commercial email marketing, requiring clear identification of the sender, offering an unsubscribe option, and honoring unsubscribe requests.

15. What is a key challenge associated with private sector data collection in the digital age?

* A. Difficulty in understanding the legal framework

* B. Lack of awareness among consumers about privacy rights

* C. Rapid technological advancements and emerging data collection methods

* D. All of the above

Answer: D**

Explanation: All of these options present challenges: legal frameworks need continual updates, consumers may not be fully aware of their rights, and new technologies require adaptation in regulations and enforcement.

16. Why is data aggregation and secondary use a concern in terms of privacy?

* A. Data aggregators often lack proper security measures.

* B. Combining data sets can reveal more personal information than individual sources.

* C. Consumers rarely consent to all potential uses of their data after aggregation.

* D. All of the above

Answer: D**

Explanation: Combining data from various sources can create detailed profiles, raising concerns about potential misuse and difficulty obtaining informed consent for all potential uses.

17. What is an ongoing challenge regarding cross-border data flows in the context of private sector data collection?

* A. Lack of internet connectivity in developing countries

* B. Differences in data privacy regulations between countries

* C. Difficulty in identifying the location of data storage

* D. All of the above

Answer: B**

Explanation: Countries have varying data privacy regulations, creating complexities when data collected in one country is transferred and stored in another with potentially weaker privacy protections.

18. How can individuals best protect their privacy in the digital age?

* A. Avoid using online services altogether.

* B. Be mindful of the information they share online.

* C. Never consent to data collection practices.

* D. Rely solely on companies' privacy policies for protection.

Answer: B**

Explanation: While complete avoidance isn't feasible in today's world, individuals can be cautious about the information they share online, understand and manage privacy settings, and exercise their rights under relevant regulations.

19. What is the primary purpose of the Children's Online Privacy Protection Act (COPPA)?

A. To regulate the content available to children online.

B. To ensure all websites are child-friendly and educational.

C. To protect the privacy of children under 13 by regulating online data collection.

D. To require parental consent for any online activity involving children.

Answer: C

Explanation: COPPA specifically focuses on protecting the privacy of children under 13 by requiring verifiable parental consent before websites and online services can collect, use, or disclose their personal information.

20. What is the main difference between the FTC Safeguards Rule and the Privacy Rule under GLBA?

A. The Safeguards Rule applies to financial institutions, while the Privacy Rule applies to all businesses.

B. The Safeguards Rule focuses on data security, while the Privacy Rule focuses on data disclosure.

C. The Safeguards Rule is for online data, while the Privacy Rule covers offline data as well.

D. The Safeguards Rule and Privacy Rule have no significant differences.

Answer: B

Explanation: Both rules fall under GLBA, but they have distinct focuses. The Safeguards Rule emphasizes implementing comprehensive security measures to protect customer financial information, while the Privacy Rule outlines requirements for financial institutions regarding informing customers about their data collection practices and providing them with choices and control over their information.

21. What is the significance of "notice and consent" regarding data collection practices?

A. Companies are required to inform users about data collection only if they plan to sell the data.

B. Individuals have the right to be informed about what data is collected and how it will be used before consenting.

C. Websites and apps must obtain consent from all users, regardless of age or location.

D. Notice and consent only apply to data collected through online forms.

Answer: B

Explanation: The principle of "notice and consent" is fundamental to fair data collection practices. Individuals have the right to be informed about what data is collected, how it will be used, and with whom it will be shared, allowing them to make informed choices about whether or not to consent.

22. Under HIPAA, what qualifies as a "covered entity"?

A. All healthcare providers, regardless of size or location.

B. Healthcare providers who accept insurance payments.

C. Healthcare providers who electronically transmit patient information.

D. Hospitals and clinics only, not individual healthcare professionals.

Answer: C

Explanation: HIPAA applies specifically to "covered entities," which include healthcare providers, health plans, and healthcare clearinghouses that transmit standard healthcare transactions electronically. Not all healthcare providers fall under this definition; for example, a solo practitioner who only keeps paper records wouldn't be considered a covered entity.

23. What type of information does the Fair Credit Reporting Act (FCRA) regulate?

A. All personal information about individuals used in any context.

B. Data collected by social media platforms for advertising purposes.

C. Publicly available information like educational achievements or employment history.

D. Information collected by credit reporting agencies used to determine creditworthiness.

Answer: D

Explanation: The FCRA focuses on the accuracy and fairness of information used by credit reporting agencies to assess an individual's creditworthiness. It doesn't apply to all personal information or data unrelated to credit history and financial standing.

24. What is an example of a situation where a school may disclose student education records under FERPA without parental consent?

A. To share the student's grades with a college admissions committee.

B. To promote the school's academic achievements using student names and photos.

C. To report suspected drug use by a student to local law enforcement.

D. To allow a private company to conduct research on student learning styles.

Answer: C

Explanation: FERPA allows exceptions for reporting suspected threats to the health or safety of the student or others, including situations involving drug use, to ensure the well-being of the school community.

25. How does the Telephone Consumer Protection Act (TCPA) restrict unsolicited telemarketing calls?

A. It completely prohibits all telemarketing calls to residential phone lines.

B. It requires telemarketers to obtain prior written consent before calling individuals.

C. It limits the number of telemarketing calls a person can receive per day.

D. It allows individuals to opt-out of telemarketing calls by adding their number to a national registry.

Answer: B

Explanation: The TCPA doesn't ban all telemarketing calls but requires prior written consent from consumers before using automated

26. What does the CAN-SPAM Act require of companies sending commercial emails?

A. To use specific marketing language and phrases in email subject lines.

B. To offer a clear and easy-to-use unsubscribe option in all commercial emails.

C. To obtain email addresses directly from individuals they intend to target.

D. To pay a registration fee to the government for every commercial email sent.

Answer: B

Explanation: The CAN-SPAM Act outlines several requirements for commercial email marketing, including providing a clear and readily available unsubscribe mechanism in all emails and honoring those unsubscribe requests within a reasonable timeframe.

27. What is a significant challenge in regulating private sector data collection in the digital age?

A. The lack of public interest in data privacy issues.

B. The difficulty in enforcing regulations across different online platforms.

C. The rapid emergence of new technologies that collect and utilize data.

D. The high cost of implementing data security measures for businesses.

Answer: C

Explanation: The constant evolution of technology and the emergence of new data collection methods pose a significant challenge to regulators. Existing regulations may not address novel data collection practices, necessitating ongoing adaptation and updates.

28. Why is data aggregation concerning from a privacy perspective?

A. Aggregated data is always used for targeted advertising purposes.

B. The process of aggregating data is inherently insecure and risky.

C. Individuals rarely have control over how their data is used after aggregation.

D. Aggregated data sets are often inaccurate and unreliable.

Answer: C

Explanation: Combining data from various sources can create detailed profiles of individuals, raising concerns that the aggregated data may be used for unforeseen purposes beyond what individuals originally consented to when their data was collected from individual sources.

29. What is an example of a cross-border data flow issue in the context of private sector data collection?

A. A social media platform collects user data from all over the world but stores it in one centralized location.

B. An e-commerce website personalizes product recommendations based on a user's location.

C. A healthcare provider shares patient information with a specialist located in another country.

D. A company uses cookies to track user activity on their website.

Answer: A

Explanation: When data collected in one country is transferred and stored in another, it raises concerns about the potential application of different data privacy regulations and the level of protection afforded to the data in the storage country.

30. What are some ways individuals can protect their privacy online?

A. Using strong passwords and enabling two-factor authentication on accounts.

B. Being cautious about the information they share online and adjusting privacy settings.

C. Regularly reviewing and updating privacy preferences on websites and apps.

D. All of the above

Answer: D

Explanation: Individuals can take various steps to protect their privacy online, including using strong passwords and enabling multi-factor authentication, being mindful of the information they share and adjusting privacy settings on platforms they use, and regularly reviewing and updating their preferences to ensure they reflect their desired level of data sharing.

Chapter 6: Government and Court Access to Private Sector Information

The balance between national security and individual privacy is a complex and often evolving issue. While governments have a legitimate interest in investigating potential threats and enforcing the law, individuals also have fundamental rights to privacy and protection from unreasonable search and seizure. This chapter explores the legal frameworks and ongoing debates surrounding government and court access to private sector information.

6.1 Law Enforcement and Privacy

Law enforcement agencies rely on various methods to gather information for investigations and prosecutions. Accessing private sector information plays a crucial role in these processes, raising concerns about potential privacy violations. Here are some key aspects to consider:

Warrants: The Fourth Amendment to the U.S. Constitution safeguards against unreasonable searches and seizures. Generally, law enforcement requires a warrant issued by a judge based on probable cause to access private sector information, such as phone records, email content, or location data.

Exceptions: There are exceptions to the warrant requirement in specific situations, such as:

Exigent circumstances: When there is an immediate threat to life or safety, law enforcement may act without a warrant to prevent harm.

Plain view doctrine: If evidence is in plain view of law enforcement officers who are lawfully in a place, no warrant is needed to seize it.

Consent searches: Individuals can voluntarily consent to a search, waiving their Fourth Amendment protections.

6.2 Legal Tools for Law Enforcement Access:

Several legal tools enable law enforcement to access private sector information, with varying levels of judicial oversight:

Subpoenas: A court order compelling the production of documents or testimony for an investigation or legal proceeding. Subpoenas issued for information from a third party, such as a telecommunications company, typically require a lower standard than a warrant, balancing law enforcement needs with privacy concerns.

National Security Letters (NSLs): Issued by the FBI under the Foreign Intelligence Surveillance Act (FISA), NSLs can compel businesses to disclose certain customer information related to foreign intelligence investigations. Critics raise concerns about the lack of judicial oversight and potential for abuse.

Gag orders: Courts may issue gag orders prohibiting individuals or entities from disclosing information about a government investigation, including the existence of a subpoena or NSL. This can raise transparency concerns and limit public scrutiny of government surveillance practices.

6.3 Privacy Concerns and Balancing the Interests:

While law enforcement tools facilitate investigations, potential privacy infringements raise ethical and legal concerns:

Scope creep: The extent to which government surveillance programs collect and retain data beyond what is necessary to pursue legitimate objectives.

Chilling effect: Individuals may be discouraged from exercising their rights freely, such as expressing dissent, fearing government monitoring.

Discrimination: Unequal application of surveillance tools based on factors like race, religion, or political beliefs.

Balancing law enforcement needs with individual privacy requires ongoing public discourse, legislative oversight, and judicial review.

6.4 National Security and Privacy

National security concerns often raise complex questions regarding the permissible level of government access to private sector information. Key considerations include:

Surveillance programs: The government may employ various surveillance programs, such as collecting bulk metadata on communications or using facial recognition technology, aiming to identify potential threats. However, these programs raise concerns about the scope, intrusiveness, and potential for misuse.

Foreign Intelligence Surveillance Act (FISA): This legislation establishes a special court for reviewing government requests for surveillance in foreign intelligence investigations. However, criticisms surround the secrecy surrounding FISA proceedings and the potential for inadequate oversight.

Executive Orders: Presidents may issue executive orders authorizing surveillance programs, sometimes raising concerns about the bypass of Congressional oversight and judicial review.

6.5 Balancing National Security and Privacy:

Similar to the concerns with law enforcement access, national security considerations require careful balancing with individual privacy:

Transparency and accountability: Clearer guidelines and increased transparency regarding the scope and limitations of government surveillance programs are crucial.

Independent oversight: Robust and independent oversight mechanisms, including judicial review and public scrutiny, are essential to ensure accountability and prevent abuses.

Proportionality: The level of intrusion into individual privacy should be proportional to the security threat being addressed.

6.6 Civil Litigation and Privacy

In civil litigation, parties may need to access private sector information held by third parties, such as financial records or medical data, to support their claims or defenses. This raises concerns about balancing the need for fair adjudication with individual privacy.

Discovery process: During the pre-trial discovery process, parties can request relevant information from each other and from third parties. However, courts may restrict discovery requests if the information sought is unduly burdensome, harassing, or irrelevant to the case.

Protective orders: Courts can issue protective orders to safeguard sensitive information disclosed during litigation, limiting its use and dissemination to prevent unauthorized disclosure.

6.6 Balancing interests:

The balance between the need for efficient and fair litigation and individual privacy requires a multifaceted approach:

Balancing tests: Courts utilize balancing tests, weighing the relevance of the information sought against the privacy interests at stake. This allows for tailored decisions based on the specific circumstances of each case.

Data minimization: The principle of data minimization encourages collecting and utilizing only the minimum amount of information necessary to achieve the legitimate purpose, reducing the potential impact on privacy.

Technological solutions: Technological solutions, such as anonymization or pseudonymization, can help protect sensitive information while still allowing relevant data to be used in litigation.

6.7 Emerging Issues and the Future

The landscape of government and court access to private sector information is constantly evolving with advancements in technology and the emergence of new data collection methods:

Big data and analytics: The ability to analyze vast amounts of data raises concerns about potential misuse and the need for robust privacy safeguards.

Cloud computing: Storing data in the cloud raises questions about jurisdiction and the ability of governments to access data stored in different countries.

Internet of Things (IoT): The proliferation of interconnected devices collecting and transmitting data presents new challenges regarding data ownership, access, and privacy rights.

Addressing these emerging issues requires ongoing collaboration between policymakers, technologists, legal experts, and civil society to ensure an appropriate balance between national security, law enforcement efficiency, and individual privacy in the digital age.

The tension between government access to private sector information and individual privacy is a complex issue with no easy answers. Striking a balance requires a nuanced understanding of the competing interests, robust legal frameworks, and ongoing efforts to ensure transparency, accountability, and respect for fundamental rights in the ever-evolving digital landscape.

Practice Question and Answers

Which constitutional amendment safeguards against unreasonable search and seizure?

A. First Amendment

B. Second Amendment

C. Fourth Amendment

D. Fifth Amendment

Answer: C

Explanation: The Fourth Amendment is the foundation for privacy protections against unreasonable government intrusion, generally requiring law enforcement to obtain a warrant.

What legal standard must generally be met for law enforcement to obtain a warrant?

A. Mere suspicion

B. Probable cause

C. Beyond a reasonable doubt

D. Absolute certainty

Answer: B

Explanation: Probable cause exists when there are enough facts and circumstances to lead a reasonable person to believe that evidence of a crime will be found. It's a higher standard than suspicion, but less strict than the proof required for a conviction.

Which is an example of an exception to the warrant requirement under the Fourth Amendment?

A. Consent to search

B. A routine traffic stop

C. A subpoena for customer records

D. All of the above

Answer: A

Explanation: Individuals may voluntarily consent to a search, waiving their Fourth Amendment rights. Other exceptions include exigent circumstances and the plain view doctrine.

Subpoenas, as compared to warrants, generally require a ______________ standard.

A. Higher

B. Lower

C. Similar

D. Subpoenas do not require a court order

Answer: B

Explanation: Subpoenas compel the production of documents or testimony but typically demonstrate a lower standard than warrants, balancing privacy with investigative needs.

What is the controversy surrounding National Security Letters (NSLs)?

A. They can only be used to investigate domestic terrorism.

B. They require a warrant issued by a judge.

C. They may contain gag orders preventing disclosure.

D. No controversies exist with the use of NSLs.

Answer: C

Explanation: NSLs can compel businesses to provide information for national security investigations, sometimes with accompanying gag orders. Critics argue this restricts transparency and can lead to overreach.

The use of government surveillance programs often raises concerns about the potential for what?

A. Inefficiency in identifying targets

B. Limited scope of their surveillance capabilities

C. Scope creep and privacy infringements

D. Public approval of government actions

Answer: C

Explanation: Surveillance programs may amass data beyond the original goals, infringing on privacy and raising concerns about potential misuse or unintended consequences.

Which legislation established a specialized court to review government requests for surveillance in foreign intelligence investigations?

A. PATRIOT Act

B. Foreign Intelligence Surveillance Act (FISA)

C. Computer Fraud and Abuse Act

D. Freedom of Information Act (FOIA)

Answer: B

Explanation: FISA created a special court (FISC) to streamline the process for approving surveillance requests in national security investigations.

Executive Orders issued by presidents sometimes authorize surveillance programs. Why can they be controversial?

A. They bypass Congressional oversight and judicial review.

B. They are generally ineffective in detecting threats.

C. They are always approved by the Supreme Court.

D. They lack public support.

Answer: A

Explanation: Executive orders may create programs without going through the traditional legislative process, leading to a lack of checks and balances.

During which phase of a civil lawsuit are parties allowed to seek information from one another and from third parties?

A. Discovery process

B. Jury selection

C. Sentencing phase

D. Appeals process

Answer: A

Explanation: The discovery process enables parties to gather relevant information to build their case, including accessing information from non-party sources.

What is the purpose of a protective order in civil litigation?

A. To expedite the discovery process

B. To protect the privacy of sensitive information disclosed during the case.

C. To limit the number of witnesses allowed to testify.

D. To determine the appropriate venue for the case.

Answer: B

Explanation: Protective orders limit the use and dissemination of sensitive information disclosed during litigation to prevent unauthorized disclosure and safeguard individual privacy.

What legal test do courts often use to balance the need for information in civil litigation with the privacy interests of individuals?

A. Means-ends test

B. Precedent test

C. Balancing test

D. Hearsay rule

Answer: C

Explanation: Balancing tests weigh the relevance and necessity of the information sought against the potential harm to privacy interests, ensuring fair litigation while protecting individual rights.

What is a potential concern regarding "big data" and analytics in the context of privacy?

A. Its focus on large datasets can miss important individual details.

B. It is slow and inefficient for analyzing information.

C. It can be used to create detailed profiles on individuals, raising privacy concerns.

D. It is primarily used for scientific research and not relevant to privacy.

Answer: C

Explanation: The ability to analyze vast amounts of data can reveal personal information and hidden patterns, raising concerns about profiling and potential misuse.

Why does cloud computing present challenges for balancing privacy concerns and government access to data?

A. Cloud storage is inherently insecure and vulnerable to breaches.

B. Data stored in the cloud may be subject to the laws of different countries, creating jurisdictional complexities.

C. Cloud providers often lack transparency about their data security practices.

D. All of the above.

Answer: B

Explanation: Data stored in the cloud might be subject to the laws of the country where the server is located, potentially hindering access by the government of the individual's home country and raising concerns about inconsistent privacy protections.

What is a potential privacy concern associated with the Internet of Things (IoT)?

A. IoT devices are generally too expensive for widespread use.

B. They do not collect or transmit any personal data.

C. The vast number of interconnected devices can create a complex web of data collection, making it difficult to track ownership and access.

D. They lack adequate security measures, making them vulnerable to hacking.

Answer: C

Explanation: The proliferation of interconnected devices collecting and transmitting data raises concerns about who owns the data, who can access it, and how it is used, potentially impacting individual privacy.

What are some key legal tools law enforcement agencies use to access private sector information?

A. Subpoenas and warrants

B. National Security Letters and gag orders

C. Data mining algorithms and facial recognition technology

D. All of the above

Answer: D

Explanation: The answer encompasses all options, highlighting the various tools used by law enforcement, each with different levels of judicial oversight and potential privacy implications.

What are some critical considerations in balancing law enforcement needs with individual privacy?

A. Ensuring law enforcement agencies have unlimited access to data.

B. Prioritizing national security interests over individual privacy concerns.

C. Striking a balance between effective law enforcement and safeguarding fundamental rights.

D. Implementing surveillance programs without public scrutiny.

Answer: C

Explanation: The chapter emphasizes the importance of achieving a balance between protecting individual privacy and enabling law enforcement to fulfill its duties effectively.

What are some potential concerns regarding the use of government surveillance programs for national security purposes?

A. They may be ineffective in preventing threats.

B. They can be costly to implement and

profile picture

complete question 18 and continue

What are some potential concerns regarding the use of government surveillance programs for national security purposes?

A. They may be ineffective in preventing threats.

B. They can be costly to implement and maintain.

C. They may lead to "scope creep" and collect more data than necessary.

D. All of the above.

Answer: D**

Explanation: All of the options represent potential concerns with government surveillance programs:

* Their effectiveness in preventing threats is debatable and subject to ongoing scrutiny.

* Implementing and maintaining large-scale surveillance programs can be financially demanding.

* "Scope creep" refers to the potential for programs to collect data beyond the initial purpose, raising privacy concerns and potentially infringing on individual rights.

What is the Foreign Intelligence Surveillance Act (FISA) and why is it controversial?

A. It outlines privacy protections for individuals under government surveillance.

B. It establishes a special court for reviewing foreign intelligence surveillance requests.

C. It grants law enforcement agencies broad powers to access private data without warrants.

D. It is widely considered an effective tool for national security without privacy concerns.

Answer: B

Explanation: FISA established the Foreign Intelligence Surveillance Court (FISC) to review government requests for surveillance in foreign intelligence investigations. The controversy surrounds the secrecy surrounding FISA proceedings and concerns about the potential for inadequate oversight and potential for abuse, despite its role in obtaining warrants for national security investigations.

What is the difference between a subpoena and a warrant in the context of accessing private sector information?

A. Warrants require probable cause, while subpoenas do not.

B. Subpoenas are used for criminal investigations, while warrants are for civil matters.

C. Warrants are issued by judges, while subpoenas are issued by law enforcement.

D. Subpoenas and warrants provide identical levels of judicial oversight.

Answer: A

Explanation: Warrants require a higher standard of probable cause to be approved by a judge, while subpoenas typically require a lower standard, balancing law enforcement needs with privacy concerns. Both involve some level of judicial oversight, but the warrant process offers a stronger check on potential government overreach.

What is the principle of data minimization and how does it relate to balancing privacy interests?

A. It encourages collecting and analyzing large data sets for more comprehensive insights.

B. It prioritizes efficiency in litigation over safeguarding sensitive information.

C. It emphasizes collecting and using only the minimum amount of data necessary to achieve a legitimate purpose, reducing privacy risks.

D. It allows individuals to opt out of providing their data for civil lawsuits.

Answer: C

Explanation: The principle of data minimization aims to strike a balance by encouraging the collection and use of only the minimum amount of information necessary for the intended purpose, reducing the potential impact on individual privacy.

What are some potential challenges in applying balancing tests when determining access to private sector information in civil litigation?

A. Balancing tests are always straightforward and easy to apply.

B. Subjectivity can influence the weight given to privacy interests versus the need for information.

C. Balancing tests are only used in criminal cases, not civil litigation.

D. There are no established legal frameworks for conducting these tests.

Answer: B

Explanation: Balancing tests involve weighing competing interests, and the weight given to each side can be subjective, potentially leading to challenges in reaching consistent decisions.

Why is the rise of "big data" a concern for individual privacy?

A. Big data analysis is primarily used for scientific research and does not involve personal information.

B. The ability to analyze vast amounts of data can reveal hidden patterns and personal information, potentially leading to profiling and discrimination.

C. Big data sets are often inaccurate and unreliable, making them unsuitable for drawing conclusions.

D. Big data analysis is too slow and inefficient for practical use.

Answer: B

Explanation: The ability to analyze vast amounts of data can reveal patterns and personal details, raising concerns about the potential for profiling individuals and misuse of this information for targeted advertising, discrimination, or other purposes.

What are some potential challenges associated with cloud computing and privacy?

A. Cloud storage ensures complete security and prevents data breaches.

B. Data stored in the cloud may be subject to the laws of different countries, creating jurisdictional complexities for access and privacy protections.

C. Cloud providers always disclose their data security practices transparently.

D. Encryption makes cloud storage completely resistant to unauthorized access.

Answer: B

Explanation: Data stored in the cloud might be subject to the laws of the country where the server is located, potentially hindering access by the government of the individual's home country and raising concerns about inconsistent privacy protections. Additionally, the lack of transparency about data security practices in some cloud providers can be concerning.

What are some potential security risks associated with the Internet of Things (IoT)?

A. All IoT devices are inherently secure and cannot be hacked.

B. Weak security measures in some devices can leave them vulnerable to hacking and unauthorized access.

C. They are too expensive to be widely adopted and pose minimal risk.

D. They do not collect or transmit any data, so there are no security concerns.

Answer: B

Explanation: The proliferation of interconnected devices, some with weak security measures, can create vulnerabilities that hackers can exploit to access and manipulate data, raising security and privacy concerns.

What are some ethical considerations regarding government access to private sector information?

A. Balancing the need for security with individual privacy and ensuring transparency.

B. Prioritizing national security interests over ethical concerns at all costs.

C. Granting law enforcement agencies unfettered access to any information they request.

D. Implementing surveillance programs without public scrutiny or oversight.

Answer: A

Explanation: Finding a balance between security needs and individual privacy while maintaining transparency and accountability are crucial ethical considerations when discussing government access to private sector information.

According to the chapter, what are some potential consequences of failing to strike a balance between national security and individual privacy?

A. It may lead to increased public trust in government agencies.

B. It can discourage individuals from exercising their fundamental rights.

C. It strengthens national security by allowing for comprehensive surveillance.

D. It guarantees individual privacy at the expense of national security.

Answer: B

Explanation: Failing to strike a balance can lead to individuals feeling discouraged from exercising

What role do technological solutions play in balancing privacy and access to information in civil litigation?

A. Technological solutions eliminate the need for balancing tests and prioritize access to information.

B. These solutions can help protect sensitive information while allowing relevant data to be used in litigation, potentially aiding the balancing process.

C. They are not relevant to civil litigation and primarily used in criminal investigations.

D. Technological solutions always favor individual privacy over the need for information disclosure.

Answer: B

Explanation: Technological solutions, such as anonymization or pseudonymization, can help protect sensitive information while still allowing relevant data to be used in litigation, contributing to a more balanced approach.

What is the role of public discourse in addressing the challenges of balancing national security and individual privacy?

A. Public discourse is unnecessary as these are complex legal matters best left to experts.

B. Open discussions can help raise awareness, encourage diverse perspectives, and foster informed decision-making.

C. Public opinion should not influence policy decisions regarding national security.

D. Public discourse is only relevant to issues of civil litigation, not national security.

Answer: B

Explanation: Public discourse allows for diverse perspectives to be heard, raising awareness and fostering informed decision-making regarding the complex balance between national security and individual privacy.

Additional Practice Questions:

What is the Electronic Communications Privacy Act (ECPA)?

Explain the concept of "chilling effect" in the context of government surveillance.

What are some arguments in favor of and against the use of facial recognition technology by law enforcement?

How does the European Union's General Data Protection Regulation (GDPR) differ from the approach to data privacy in the United States?

What are some potential benefits and risks associated with using data anonymization techniques?

Chapter 7: Workplace Privacy

Introduction to Workplace Privacy

The workplace is an environment where individuals dedicate a significant portion of their time and energy. While employers have legitimate interests in ensuring productivity and maintaining a professional environment, employees also have fundamental rights to privacy. This chapter explores the complex and evolving landscape of workplace privacy, examining the legal and ethical considerations surrounding various aspects of the employer-employee relationship.

Key Concepts and Definitions:

Workplace privacy: Refers to the expectation of an individual to maintain a certain level of privacy regarding their personal information, communications, and activities within the workplace.

Reasonable expectation of privacy: A subjective legal standard that considers various factors, including the nature of the information, the context in which it was collected, and the employee's efforts to maintain privacy.

Monitoring: The act of collecting and recording information about an employee's activities, such as email, internet usage, phone calls, or physical location.

Surveillance: A broader term encompassing various monitoring practices, often associated with a more intrusive or covert nature.

Balancing Interests:

Balancing the legitimate interests of both employers and employees is crucial in navigating workplace privacy issues. Here are some key considerations:

Employer interests:

Maintaining a safe and productive work environment.

Preventing misconduct or illegal activities.

Protecting business assets and confidential information.

Employee interests:

Maintaining a sense of personal autonomy and control over their information and activities.

Protecting their personal lives and communications from unnecessary intrusion.

Avoiding discrimination or unfair treatment based on personal information.

Privacy Before, During, and After Employment:

Workplace privacy considerations can be broadly categorized into three phases:

1. Pre-employment:

Background checks: Employers often conduct background checks on potential employees, but they must comply with relevant laws and regulations, ensuring fairness and avoiding discriminatory practices.

Drug testing: Depending on the industry and specific circumstances, drug testing may be permissible, but it's subject to legal requirements and ethical considerations regarding privacy and potential discrimination.

2. During employment:

Monitoring: Various forms of monitoring are prevalent in workplaces, including email, internet usage, phone calls, video surveillance, and GPS tracking. The legality and ethical implications of these practices depend on factors like the type of monitoring, its purpose, whether it is disclosed to employees, and the level of intrusiveness.

Access to personal devices: Employers may have policies regarding employee use of personal devices for work purposes, raising questions about potential access to personal information and the need for clear boundaries.

Social media: Off-duty social media activity generally falls outside the scope of workplace privacy, but employers may have policies regarding online conduct that could impact the workplace or the organization's reputation.

3. Post-employment:

Retention and disposal of employee data: Employers have a responsibility to retain and dispose of employee data in accordance with relevant laws and regulations, respecting individuals' privacy rights even after employment ends.

Non-compete agreements: These agreements restrict employees from competing with their former employer in certain ways, but they must be reasonable and enforceable under applicable law, considering the potential impact on individual career opportunities.

Practice Questions and Answers

An employer wants to conduct a background check on a job applicant. What are some legal limitations they need to consider?

A. They may gather unlimited information from any source.

B. They must comply with laws such as the Fair Credit Reporting Act.

C. There are no restrictions on what information they can gather.

D. They can only conduct background checks after they make a job offer.

Answer: B

Explanation: The Fair Credit Reporting Act (FCRA) and similar laws regulate how employers obtain and use background information, including credit reports and criminal history. Employers often need to obtain consent and may not use discriminatory information in hiring.

Under what circumstances may it be permissible for an employer to conduct drug testing on job applicants?

A. It's always permissible as part of the application process.

B. Only if the job is safety-sensitive or regulated by industry law.

C. Employers may require drug testing for all job applicants regardless of job type.

D. It's never permissible to require drug testing of applicants.

Answer: B

Explanation: It may be permissible to require drug testing for safety-sensitive jobs or where mandated by industry-specific regulations. Laws may vary among jurisdictions, and there are privacy considerations.

Which of the following forms of employee monitoring would typically be considered the LEAST intrusive?

A. Video surveillance in a lunchroom

B. Monitoring keystrokes and website visits.

C. Reviewing an employee's company-issued email inbox.

D. GPS tracking of company vehicles.

Answer: A

Explanation: Video surveillance in a common area like a lunchroom is generally less intrusive than monitoring an individual's work product or location. Still, notice and purpose are relevant factors.

An employee believes their employer has been reading their personal emails sent from a company computer. What legal considerations are involved in this scenario?

A. Employers have the right to monitor all electronic communications on their systems.

B. Personal emails always enjoy complete privacy protection.

C. Employee expectations of privacy and company policies are key factors.

D. Only law enforcement can access email content, even on company systems.

Answer: C

Explanation: While companies often have broad monitoring rights, employees might have some reasonable expectation of privacy regarding personal emails. Clear company policies and employee notification are key to manage expectations.

What is a potential concern with employers having policies about employee social media activity outside of work hours?

A. Social media posts can never be relevant to employment decisions.

B. It might limit employees' freedom of expression if overly broad.

C. Employers have no interest in limiting employees' social media use.

D. Companies often need more stringent controls over online activity.

Answer: B

Explanation: While employers have legitimate interests in protecting reputation and addressing workplace impact, overly broad social media policies could infringe on employee free speech rights if not carefully crafted.

What are an employer's responsibilities after an employee leaves the company?

A. Store all employee data indefinitely for future reference.

B. Disclose all collected employee information in response to any request.

C. Dispose of employee data in accordance with privacy laws and regulations.

D. Maintain complete secrecy of former employees' information at all times.

Answer: C

Explanation: Employers have responsibilities regarding the secure disposal of employee data to prevent unauthorized access, with timeframes often dictated by regulations.

Let me know if you'd like more questions, or ones in a specific area!

An employer wants to install video surveillance cameras in the workplace. What factors should they consider to ensure they are balancing their legitimate interests with employee privacy expectations?

A. Only focus on the employer's need for security and efficiency.

B. Install cameras in all areas of the workplace without informing employees.

C. Consider the nature of the work environment, the purpose of the surveillance, its intrusiveness, and inform employees clearly.

D. Prioritize employee privacy concerns above all else, even if it hinders security.

Answer: C

Explanation: Striking a balance requires considering the purpose and intrusiveness of the monitoring, the nature of the workplace, and informing employees clearly about the monitoring practices. Transparency and a legitimate purpose are crucial.

What are potential consequences of failing to balance employer and employee interests in the context of workplace privacy?

A. It may lead to increased employee morale and productivity.

B. It could lead to decreased employee trust, lower morale, and potential legal challenges.

C. It has no significant impact on either employers or employees.

D. Employees are always solely responsible for protecting their privacy in the workplace.

Answer: B

Explanation: Failing to balance interests can lead to employee dissatisfaction, decreased trust, and potential legal challenges arising from privacy violations.

An employer discovers an employee is using company resources for personal tasks during work hours. What are some ethical considerations involved in addressing this situation?

A. Publicly reprimand the employee to deter others.

B. Focus solely on enforcing company policies without considering mitigating factors.

C. Consider the severity of the offense, potential reasons behind the behavior, and address it in a fair and confidential manner.

D. Implementing strict monitoring practices is the only ethical approach to address such situations.

Answer: C

Explanation: Addressing the situation fairly and confidentially, considering extenuating circumstances, and focusing on correcting the behavior rather than public shaming are key ethical considerations.

Why is it important to stay updated on evolving laws and regulations related to workplace privacy?

A. These laws and regulations rarely change and have minimal impact on workplaces.

B. Keeping up-to-date ensures employers can implement more intrusive monitoring practices.

C. Staying informed allows both employers and employees to understand their rights and responsibilities, and helps navigate compliance challenges.

D. Only legal professionals need to be aware of the latest legal developments.

Answer: C

Explanation: Legal and regulatory landscapes evolve, and staying informed ensures both employers and employees understand their rights and obligations, promoting compliance and avoiding potential risks.

Chapter 8: State Privacy Laws

In the United States, the legal landscape regarding data privacy is characterized by a complex interplay between federal and state laws. While the federal government has enacted some broad privacy regulations, individual states have increasingly taken the lead in creating more comprehensive and specific legislation. This chapter delves into the evolving world of state privacy laws, exploring their key components and their potential impact on businesses and individuals.

Federal vs. State Authority:

The legal foundation for data privacy in the United States originates from a combination of federal laws and state regulations. However, there is no single, overarching federal data privacy law similar to the European Union's General Data Protection Regulation (GDPR). Instead, various federal statutes address specific aspects of data privacy, such as:

Sector-specific regulations: Laws like the Gramm-Leach-Bliley Act (GLBA) for financial institutions and the Health Insurance Portability and Accountability Act (HIPAA) for healthcare data impose data security and privacy requirements on specific industries.

Consumer protection laws: The Fair Credit Reporting Act (FCRA) regulates the collection, use, and disclosure of consumer credit information, while the Children's Online Privacy Protection Act (COPPA) protects the privacy of children online.

Fourth Amendment: The Fourth Amendment to the U.S. Constitution protects individuals from unreasonable search and seizure, which has been interpreted to offer some privacy protections in specific contexts.

However, these federal regulations often leave gaps and lack the comprehensive approach found in some state laws. This has led to a growing trend of states enacting their own privacy laws, aiming to address specific concerns and provide greater individual control over personal information.

Financial Data:

One area where state privacy laws have gained significant traction is the regulation of financial data. Following the national data breach at a major credit reporting agency in 2017, several states enacted laws expanding individual rights concerning their financial data. These laws often include:

Right to access: Individuals have the right to access their personal financial information held by companies.

Right to correction: Individuals can request corrections to inaccurate or incomplete information.

Right to deletion: In some cases, individuals can request the deletion of their data under certain circumstances.

Opt-out of data sharing: Individuals can choose not to have their information sold or shared with third parties.

These rights empower individuals to understand and control the use of their financial data, adding an extra layer of protection beyond existing federal regulations.

Data Security:

While data security is not solely addressed by state privacy laws, many states have included provisions requiring covered entities to implement and maintain reasonable security measures to protect personal information from unauthorized access, disclosure, alteration, or destruction. This aligns with the increasing focus on data security best practices in the digital age.

Data Breach Notification Laws:

Data breaches can expose sensitive personal information and lead to significant harm for individuals. Recognizing this risk, many states have enacted data breach notification laws requiring covered entities to notify individuals and potentially regulators in the event of a data breach. These laws typically specify:

Trigger thresholds: The size and type of data breach that necessitates notification.

Notification timeframes: The timeframe within which affected individuals must be notified.

Content of notification: The information that must be included in the notification, such as the nature of the breach and potential risks to individuals.

By requiring timely notification, these laws empower individuals to take steps to protect themselves from identity theft and fraud, promoting accountability for data security practices.

Marketing Laws:

Marketing practices, particularly those involving targeted advertising and the use of personal data, are another area where state privacy laws are evolving. Some states have enacted laws addressing concerns like:

Do Not Track (DNT) signals: These laws may require companies to respect user-generated DNT signals instructing them not to track online browsing activity.

Targeted advertising: Some laws require transparency about how personal data is used for targeted advertising and provide individuals with opt-out options.

Sale of personal information: Certain state laws give individuals the right to opt-out of the sale of their personal information.

These measures aim to provide individuals with greater control over how their data is used for marketing purposes, potentially restricting intrusive practices and offering more choices.

Challenges and Considerations:

The increasing patchwork of state privacy laws presents several challenges for businesses operating across multiple jurisdictions. Compliance can require navigating a complex web of regulations, potentially increasing administrative and operational burdens. Additionally, the lack of uniformity across state laws can create uncertainty and potentially hinder innovation in the data-driven economy.

Despite these challenges, the evolving landscape of state privacy laws reflects growing societal concerns about data privacy and individual control. As states continue to enact and refine their own regulations, the federal government might be prompted to consider more comprehensive data privacy legislation.

Practice Questions and Answers

What is the primary difference between federal and state privacy laws in the United States?

Answer: Federal laws focus on specific industries or types of data, while state laws often provide broader and more comprehensive privacy protections.

Explanation: The U.S. lacks a single overarching federal privacy law like the GDPR. Federal laws like HIPAA (healthcare) and GLBA (finance) provide sector-specific regulations. States are increasingly filling the gaps with broader laws offering individuals more control over their data.

Which of the following is a common right often granted by state privacy laws?

A. Right to access and obtain a copy of personal information held by a company.

B. Right to opt-out of the sale of personal information.

C. Right to sue companies for any privacy violation.

D. All of the above

Answer: D. All of the above.

Explanation: Many state laws are converging on core rights: access, opt-out of sale, and sometimes deletion. Lawsuits are an option, but the right to sue may have limitations depending on the specific law.

What is the general purpose of state data breach notification laws?

A. To punish companies that experience data breaches.

B. To enable individuals to take steps to protect themselves after a data breach.

C. To force companies to adopt perfect cybersecurity measures.

D. To prevent data breaches from happening in the first place.

Answer: B. To enable individuals to take steps to protect themselves after a data breach.

Explanation: While breaches may lead to penalties, the primary goal of these laws is to inform affected individuals so they can monitor accounts, change passwords, etc., reducing the harm caused by the breach.

The Gramm-Leach-Bliley Act (GLBA) primarily focuses on protecting the privacy of what type of data?

A. Healthcare data

B. Financial data

C. Children's online data

D. Location data

Answer: B. Financial data

Explanation: GLBA mandates that financial institutions safeguard sensitive customer information and disclose their data-sharing practices.

What is the purpose of the Children's Online Privacy Protection Act (COPPA)?

A. To protect the online privacy of children under the age of 13.

B. To regulate the collection of user data from all websites.

C. To prevent online harassment and cyberbullying.

D. To establish data security standards for all online businesses.

Answer: A. To protect the online privacy of children under the age of 13.

Explanation: COPPA requires websites and online services aimed at children to obtain parental consent before collecting personal information from children under 13.

Many state privacy laws include provisions regarding data security. What is the general purpose of these provisions?

A. To outline specific technical measures all companies must implement.

B. To punish companies for any data breach that occurs.

C. To establish a "reasonable" standard for protecting personal data.

D. To prevent any and all data breaches from happening.

Answer: C. To establish a "reasonable" standard for protecting personal data.

Explanation: Laws generally avoid overly prescriptive technical measures. They focus on whether companies acted reasonably to protect data based on the sensitivity and amount of data involved.

How might state "Do Not Track" (DNT) laws impact online marketing practices?

A. They could require companies to honor user requests to not track their online activity.

B. They would completely eliminate all forms of targeted advertising.

C. They have little impact as companies rarely track user data.

D. Their main goal is to prevent data breaches.

Answer: A. They could require companies to honor user requests to not track their online activity.

Explanation: DNT laws are often limited, requiring honoring a browser setting, and may not stop all tracking, but they offer more choice for users concerned about behavioral advertising.

How can businesses stay up-to-date on the evolving landscape of state privacy laws?

A. Ignore all state laws and focus only on federal regulations.

B. Consult with attorneys and monitor developments from state privacy agencies.

C. Wait to see if a federal privacy law is passed.

D. Assume that all states have the same privacy laws.

Answer: B. Consult with attorneys and monitor developments from state privacy agencies.

Explanation: Due to the diverse nature of state laws and their frequent updates, seeking guidance from legal professionals specializing in data privacy and keeping track of relevant state agency announcements are crucial for businesses to navigate the evolving legal landscape.

What is a potential challenge for businesses operating across multiple states with varying data privacy laws?

A. State laws generally provide less oversight and are easier to comply with.

B. Businesses can choose to follow the strictest state law and be compliant everywhere.

C. There are few practical differences in state laws and compliance is straightforward.

D. Meeting the diverse compliance requirements across different states can be complex and costly.

Answer: D. Meeting the diverse compliance requirements across different states can be complex and costly.

Explanation: Varying requirements across states can create administrative burdens and necessitate adjustments to data collection, storage, and usage practices to comply with specific state regulations.

Why might some states be more proactive in enacting their own data privacy laws?

A. They want to create additional burdens and challenges for businesses operating in their state.

B. They are concerned about the federal government's lack of action on data privacy issues.

C. They don't trust federal agencies to adequately protect the privacy of their citizens.

D. All states have the same level of enthusiasm for data privacy regulation.

Answer: B & C. They are concerned about the federal government's lack of action and might not trust their ability to adequately protect citizens' privacy.

Explanation: In the absence of strong federal legislation, states may feel compelled to act independently to address growing public concerns about data privacy and offer greater control to individuals.

Which state was the first to enact a comprehensive data privacy law in the United States?

A. California

B. New York

C. Illinois

D. Texas

Answer: A. California

Explanation: California's Consumer Privacy Act (CCPA) of 2018 was one of the first comprehensive data privacy laws enacted in the US, inspiring other states to follow suit.

What are some key rights granted to individuals under the California Consumer Privacy Act (CCPA)?

A. Right to sue companies for any privacy violation.

B. Right to know what personal data is collected about them and its purpose.

C. Right to have all their personal data deleted from a company's systems.

D. All of the above

Answer: D. All of the above

Explanation: CCPA grants individuals various rights, including the right to know, access, and delete their data, opt-out of its sale, and receive specific information about data collection practices.

What are some potential consequences for businesses found to be in violation of state privacy laws?

A. Automatic criminal charges against company executives.

B. Fines and potential civil lawsuits from individuals and state authorities.

C. Businesses may be required to shut down operations permanently.

D. There are no significant consequences for non-compliance with state privacy laws.

Answer: B. Fines and potential civil lawsuits from individuals and state authorities.

Explanation: While criminal charges are rare, non-compliance can result in significant financial penalties and legal action from individuals or state enforcement agencies.

14. What are some potential benefits of having a federal data privacy law in the United States?

A. It would weaken protection for consumers, as businesses would only need to comply with one law.

B. It could create a more unified baseline for data privacy rights across the country.

C. It would likely increase compliance costs for businesses operating in multiple states.

D. It would eliminate the need for state privacy laws and create a simpler system.

Answer: B. It could create a more unified baseline for data privacy rights across the country.

Explanation: A federal law could establish a consistent minimum standard of data privacy rights for all individuals, regardless of where they live. This would address the uneven patchwork of state laws.

15. What is a potential drawback of a federal data privacy law?

A. It may be less strict than certain existing state laws and reduce individual rights.

B. It could eliminate the need for innovation and experimentation in state privacy laws.

C. It could be more challenging for the federal government to enforce than state laws.

D. All of the above.

Answer: D. All of the above.

Explanation: A federal law may preempt stronger state laws, reducing protections. It could limit states' ability to be laboratories for stronger privacy measures, and enforcement resources could be a challenge at the federal level.

16. Companies operating in states with strict privacy laws often adopt those standards across their nationwide operations. Why might they do this?

A. They are trying to confuse consumers about their data privacy practices.

B. It makes compliance simpler and reduces legal risk.

C. They want to be subject to more lawsuits and potential regulatory penalties.

D. It is strictly required by federal law.

Answer: B. It makes compliance simpler and reduces legal risk.

Explanation: It's often easier and less risky to apply a higher standard across the board instead of tracking different rules based on the location of a user.

17. Data privacy laws increasingly focus on giving individuals the "right to be forgotten." What does this right typically entail?

A. The right to delete all personal data held by a company upon request.

B. The right to know the exact algorithms used to make decisions about them.

C. The right to never have their data stored by companies in the first place.

D. The right to transfer their data to a competing service with ease.

Answer: A. The right to delete all personal data held by a company upon request.

Explanation: While not unlimited, the "right to be forgotten" (or right to erasure) often allows individuals to request that companies delete personal data about them, with some exceptions.

18. Some states are considering privacy laws focused on regulating the use of biometric data. What is an example of biometric data?

A. An individual's website browsing history.

B. An individual's social security number.

C. An individual's facial scans or fingerprints.

D. An individual's phone location data.

Answer: C. An individual's facial scans or fingerprints.

Explanation: Biometric data includes unique physical identifiers like facial geometry, voice recordings, and fingerprints, often used for authentication purposes.

19. How might state privacy laws influence how companies design and develop new products and services?

A. Companies will no longer be able to innovate new products due to privacy regulations.

B. Companies might adopt a "privacy by design" approach, proactively considering privacy implications from the start.

C. Companies will likely focus on states with weaker privacy laws when building new products.

D. State privacy laws have no significant impact on the product development process.

Answer: B. Companies might adopt a "privacy by design" approach, proactively considering privacy implications from the start.

Explanation: Proactive privacy planning can help companies avoid costly design changes after launch due to compliance issues and build greater consumer trust.

20. What is one way individuals can stay informed about changes to state privacy laws that might affect them?

A. Regularly check the websites of state attorneys general or privacy agencies.

B. Subscribe to email newsletters from companies they do business with.

C. Become a data privacy lawyer and study the laws directly.

D. A and B.

Answer: D. A and B

Explanation: Both sources are good avenues for staying up-to-date on legal changes and understanding how your data might be used.

21. Which of the following statements is most accurate regarding the California Privacy Rights Act (CPRA)?

A. It completely replaced the CCPA, offering no additional protections for individuals.

B. It builds upon the CCPA, strengthening existing rights and adding new ones, such as the right to data portability.

C. It applies only to specific industries, such as healthcare and finance.

D. It has been struck down by courts and is not currently in effect.

Answer: B. It builds upon the CCPA, strengthening existing rights and adding new ones, such as the right to data portability.

Explanation: The CPRA, which went into effect in 2023, builds upon the CCPA by expanding the definition of personal information, strengthening consumer rights, and requiring additional transparency from businesses regarding data collection and sharing practices.

22. How does the Virginia Consumer Data Protection Act (VCDPA) differ from the CCPA in terms of the "right to opt-out" of data sales?

A. The VCDPA offers a broader right to opt-out, including the sale of derived data.

B. The CCPA only allows individuals to opt-out of the sale of personal information, not derived data.

C. Both offer the same rights regarding opting-out of data sales.

D. The VCDPA does not grant individuals the right to opt-out of data sales.

Answer: A. The VCDPA offers a broader right to opt-out, including the sale of derived data.

Explanation: While both the CCPA and VCDPA allow individuals to opt-out of the sale of personal information, the VCDPA extends this right to include derived data, which is information created or inferred from personal information.

23. What is one of the key challenges associated with complying with multiple state data breach notification laws?

A. Businesses have to notify all individuals affected by a breach, regardless of their location.

B. Different states have varying definitions of what constitutes a data breach.

C. There is no penalty for non-compliance with state data breach notification laws.

D. Businesses can ignore breach notification requirements if they comply with federal regulations.

Answer: B. Different states have varying definitions of what constitutes a data breach.

Explanation: Compliance with varying state notification laws can be complex due to different trigger thresholds (the size and type of data breach that necessitates notification) and differing definitions of what constitutes personal information requiring notification.

24. What is the primary purpose of the Utah Consumer Privacy Act (UCPA)?

A. To establish strict data security requirements for all businesses operating in the state.

B. To grant individuals broad rights to access, correct, and delete their data.

C. To create a clear and predictable legal framework for data privacy while minimizing burdens on businesses.

D. To impose significant fines on companies that violate individual privacy rights.

Answer: C. To create a clear and predictable legal framework for data privacy while minimizing burdens on businesses.

Explanation: While still offering individuals key privacy rights, the UCPA emphasizes creating a balanced approach, aiming to achieve its goals without placing excessive compliance burdens on businesses, particularly smaller companies.

25. What is the potential impact of state privacy laws on the way businesses collect and use consumer data for marketing purposes?

A. Companies will no longer be able to collect any data from consumers for marketing purposes.

B. Businesses might need to obtain explicit consent before using data for targeted advertising.

C. Companies will likely focus their marketing efforts on offline channels.

D. State privacy laws have no significant impact on marketing practices.

Answer: B. Businesses might need to obtain explicit consent before using data for targeted advertising.

Explanation: While not an outright ban, state privacy laws could require companies to obtain clear and affirmative consent from individuals before using their data for targeted advertising or other specific purposes, potentially impacting data collection practices for marketing campaigns.

Chapter 9: International Privacy Regulation

This chapter explores the complex and evolving landscape of international data privacy regulation. It delves into key issues like:

International Data Transfers: Regulations governing the transfer of personal data across national borders.

APEC Privacy Framework: A non-binding framework promoting cross-border cooperation on data privacy issues.

Cross-Border Enforcement Issues: Challenges and cooperation efforts in enforcing data privacy laws across different countries.

International Data Transfers

The increasing global interconnectedness necessitates the flow of data across borders for various purposes, including trade, communication, and cloud services. However, concerns exist regarding the potential misuse of personal data transferred internationally.

Several legal frameworks attempt to regulate international data transfers:

General Data Protection Regulation (GDPR): The EU's GDPR imposes strict requirements for transferring personal data outside the European Economic Area (EEA) to countries deemed to have "inadequate" data protection laws. These transfers require additional safeguards, such as standard contractual clauses approved by the EU or obtaining explicit consent from individuals.

Asia-Pacific Economic Cooperation (APEC) Cross-Border Privacy Rules (CBPRs): This voluntary framework helps APEC member economies establish common principles for data privacy protection and facilitate the secure flow of data across the region.

Model Contract Clauses: Standard contractual clauses developed by data protection authorities offer a mechanism for companies to ensure adequate safeguards for data transferred to countries outside their jurisdiction.

APEC Privacy Framework

The APEC Privacy Framework is a non-binding set of principles adopted by APEC economies in 2016. It aims to:

Promote transparency and accountability in data collection and use.

Allow individuals to access and correct their personal data.

Provide safeguards for cross-border data transfers.

While not legally binding, the APEC framework serves as a reference point for member economies to develop their national data privacy laws and enhance cross-border cooperation on data privacy issues.

Cross-Border Enforcement Issues

Enforcing data privacy laws across different countries presents unique challenges:

Jurisdictional issues: Determining the appropriate jurisdiction to handle data privacy violations involving individuals and businesses across different countries can be complex.

Differing enforcement mechanisms: Each country might have its own data protection authority and enforcement procedures, leading to inconsistencies and potential gaps in enforcement.

Limited international cooperation: Cooperation between national data protection authorities is crucial, but it can be hampered by differing legal systems and priorities.

Despite these challenges, efforts are underway to improve cross-border enforcement:

Mutual Legal Assistance Treaties (MLATs): Treaties facilitating cooperation between law enforcement agencies, allowing them to request assistance from each other in investigating and prosecuting data privacy violations.

Memoranda of Understanding (MOUs): Agreements between data protection authorities to share information, collaborate on investigations, and facilitate cross-border enforcement actions.

Understanding these aspects of international data privacy regulation is crucial for businesses operating globally, as they need to navigate complex legal frameworks and ensure compliance with relevant data transfer and privacy protection regulations across different jurisdictions.

Conclusion

The world of data privacy regulation is constantly evolving, driven by the ever-increasing flow of personal data across borders and the growing awareness of individuals' privacy rights. As we have seen throughout this book, navigating this complex landscape requires a comprehensive understanding of international frameworks, national laws, and emerging trends.

The future of international data privacy regulation is likely to be shaped by several key factors:

Technological advancements: New technologies, such as artificial intelligence and the Internet of Things (IoT), will continue to challenge existing legal frameworks and necessitate ongoing adaptation of data privacy regulations.

Increased regulatory convergence: While significant differences exist between national data privacy laws, there might be a trend towards greater convergence as countries seek to balance the free flow of data with the need to protect individual privacy.

The role of international organizations: International organizations, such as the APEC and the OECD, are likely to play an increasingly important role in facilitating dialogue, promoting best practices, and fostering cooperation between countries on data privacy issues.

As individuals, we can play a vital role in shaping the future of data privacy by:

Educating ourselves about our data privacy rights and understanding how our data is collected and used.

Holding organizations accountable for their data handling practices.

Supporting initiatives that promote strong and effective data privacy regulations.

By working together, we can create a future where technology serves humanity and individual privacy is respected and protected.

Understanding international data privacy regulation is crucial for businesses operating globally, policymakers seeking to establish effective legal frameworks, and individuals wanting to protect their privacy in an increasingly interconnected world. As technology continues to evolve and data flows ever more freely across borders, ongoing collaboration and innovation will be essential in ensuring a balanced approach that fosters economic growth, technological advancement, and individual privacy protection.